# It's time for trees

## A guide to species selection for the UK

### Mike Glover

Published by Barcham Trees Plc

© 2009 Barcham Trees Plc

ISBN: 978-0-9563385-0-1 Hardback

ISBN: 978-0-9563385-1-8 Paperback

# Contents

# About the author

Mike Glover graduated from Writtle Agricultural College in 1990 with a Higher National Diploma in Commercial Horticulture. The following year he was awarded the Wilfred Cave Scholarship by the Royal Bath & West Society to study 'Instant Garden Techniques' in California.

Returning to the UK, Mike took up a position with Barcham Trees, where he is now Managing Director. In 2003 he patented the Light Pot in both Europe and the UK with the aim of producing trees with sustainable root systems geared for long term transplanting success. Barcham Trees is now the largest nursery of its type in Europe.

Acknowledgements
Many thanks go to Peter Wells who has dedicated the past four years to the photography for this book. Out in all weathers and locations from dawn to dusk, his comprehensive tree knowledge has made this work possible.

Thanks also to Warren Holmes-Chatfield, our Production Director here at Barcham, for growing and presenting our trees in such a way as to make photography an enjoyable task.

# Introduction

## *Containing success*

**In a search for methods to produce a sustainable root system suitable for transplanting, Barcham Trees developed their Light Pot™ that was to give dramatic results.**

Traditions are hard to break. From the first time I planted a containerised tree I had grave doubts over the sustainability of the root system. So often a mass of fibrous and spiralled roots is applauded, but I have always thought of them as a time bomb waiting to explode.

My first experience of this was after viewing an avenue of Pinus nigra Austriaca on a roadside verge in Surrey. The trees had been planted as 4 litre, 60-90cm tall plants and by the time I saw them they had grown to over 3m in height, each supported by heavy grade stakes. Within a week of the stakes being removed the trees had fallen over and on closer inspection the old 4 litre pot volume had developed into a block of wood with three or four prongs of root protruding.

Pyrus calleryana Chanticleer at Barcham in December.

### Problem roots

The cause of this lack of anchorage started the moment the young pines were establishing in black pots. As their roots developed and reached the sides of the container they began to spiral randomly, forming a knotted and tangled root system. At secondary thickening the roots knitted ever closer and were never allowed to establish to form the anchorage that was necessary to sustain the weight of the plant above ground. Fatal results were inevitable.

Shrubs rarely attain sufficient weight above ground for this lack of anchorage to matter, but even here when a plant is pot bound (grown in the same container for over 12 months), the root system may not be adequate to support vigorous growth. However, any plant grown in a black pot that has the capacity for growing into a tree has a good chance of its life span being seriously impeded by poor root development.

As a nurseryman, growing trees in black pots that may well fail at a later date seemed pointless. My aim was to find a way of producing container tree stock that would thrive through to maturity after planting. Traditionally, trees have been lifted from the ground in the autumn and winter and delivered bare-rooted to a site where they were heeled-in and planted when possible. Typically a consignment of 200 trees delivered for planting at a new development would arrive on site having been lifted from a nursery field about a week earlier. The contractor may plant up to 25 large trees per day, so by the time the first 100 have been planted the balance could have been out of the ground for two weeks. The consequence of this is seen the following summer when the site is littered with either dead or dying trees.

Trees should be treated like fish out of water when they are handled bare-rooted, as they still have a demand for water with no means of getting it. Good husbandry lengthens the time a tree is able to survive out of the ground before planting, but for many varieties the period the tree is out of the ground is too long to ensure survival.

Root-balling trees keeps the roots moist when out of the ground, but still wounds the root system when they are lifted, placing the tree under stress from the outset. Commonly, only the thick roots remain within the root ball, with the water providing fibrous roots left behind in the field. For mycorrhizal specific genera such as Beech and Oak this can be particularly harmful, as the symbiotic relationship mainly exists on the outer reaches of the root system to enhance root-hair nutrient and water uptake. All this is left behind when a tree is root-balled or is dried off when the tree is lifted bare rooted. Hence the need for container stock. This offers ease of storage and handling as well as an unwounded root system for delivery to the site.

## Light Pots

Our answer to solve these problems came from a horticultural trial in Australia that produced a totally unintended result. There, eucalyptus growers were finding their container stock root system being scorched by the heat build up of an unrelenting sun beating down on black plastic containers. The rationale was that one wears a white t-shirt on a hot day to keep cool so why not use white pots to reflect the heat of the sun? This worked well, the pot temperature lowered, but when they looked at the root system they noticed that the roots all grew vertically down the confines of the container instead of spiralling.

The white containers allowed a small amount of light penetration into the root zone and this triggers a phototropic and geotropic reaction, in that the roots grew away from the light and obeyed the pull of gravity. When these trees were planted out the roots were not impeded by each other's growth and were able to explore the soil effectively, allowing rapid and sustained establishment.

This was the answer to our problem at Barcham. We developed a white pot, similar to an aggregate bag that could support handles and retain its integral strength all the way to the planting site, to deliver an unwounded root system fit for sustained establishment. In 2003 we developed the white pots further. We incorporated a permeable and degradable mulch mat and root barrier into the design to aid our customers planting in paved areas. We patented the design and trademarked the containers 'Light Pots'.

A non-spiralled and viable root system produced using Barcham Light Pots.
*Betula utilis Jacquemontii*

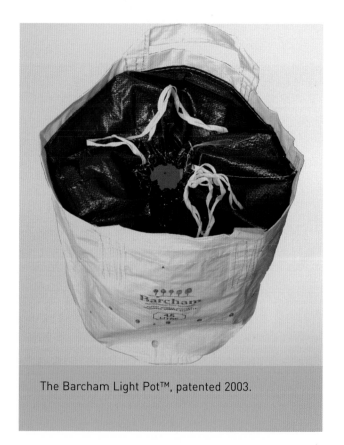

The Barcham Light Pot™, patented 2003.

● Telephone 01353 720 748 ● www.barcham.co.uk ● Fax 01353 723 060

## Shelf Life

If a tree is in the same pot for too long it doesn't matter what colour or design the container is for the root system to be no longer viable when it comes to planting. Recent research trials in Florida have shown the effects of spiralled or tangled roots and these problems have been perpetuated by potting up stock from container to container. Trees grown in this way are very susceptible to blowing over in strong winds, a regular occurrence in America, and there is now a huge backlash over there on the fallibility of nursery production methods.

At Barcham we have always containerized trees rather than container grow them. This may seem a small distinction, but it can make a huge difference to how the plant establishes long term. An outward facing radial root system is what's needed as if roots are deviated for too long they randomly knot together and as they expand with secondary thickening they girdle, leaving the tree with both poor anchorage and growth potential.

Our trees are lifted from our field unit bare rooted and then containerized into our Light Pots to re-grow a root system fit for sale some twelve months later.

Once ready for despatch, if stock remains unsold the roots continue to develop and can girdle if left for too long even though the top of the tree looks like it is still thriving. With this in mind we issue every batch of trees a bar code to monitor how long they have been in their pots and so keep track of their shelf life. It is our trick to despatch our stock before shelf life is reached but trees that go past this point are routinely culled. The shelf life is decided by genera and as far as we know we are the only nursery that manages their stock in this way.

## Track record

We have been growing and selling trees in our containers for over 20 years and our stock is now planted along the length and breadth of the UK so you will never be too far away from a Barcham Tree. My six year old claims that every tree she passes is from Barcham which is rather an overstatement but if you would like a local reference for our stock we would be pleased to point you in the right direction!

## Come and see for yourselves

I hope you enjoy this book of trees which are well suited for planting in the UK. You are most welcome to visit our nursery, by appointment, where we have over 125,000 trees in Light Pots on our 300 acre site near Ely, Cambridgeshire.

We have a great team of enthusiastic arborists who would be delighted to show you our range of stock.

Look forward to seeing you here!

Semi-mature Platanus x hispanica at Barcham in 1000 litre Light Pots.

# English to Latin Translator

Alder ............................................................Alnus & varieties
Almond ................................................................Prunus dulcis
Amur Cork Tree .....................................Phellodendron amurense
Amur Maple ...........................................................Acer ginnala
Angelica Tree............................................................Aralia elata
Antarctic Beech ........................................Nothofagus antarctica
Apple ........................................................................Malus
Ash...........................................................Fraxinus & varieties
Aspen ........................................Populus tremula & varieties
Atlas Cedar ...............................Cedrus atlantica & varieties
Austrian Pine..............................................Pinus nigra Austriaca

Bamboo..........................................Phyllostachys & varieties
Bastard Service Tree.......................Sorbus thuringiaca Fastigiata
Bay Laurel................................................Laurus nobilis
Bay Willow .............................................Salix pentandra
Beech.........................................................Fagus & varieties
Birch...........................................................Betula & varieties
Bird Cherry....................................Prunus padus & varieties
Blue Spruce .................................Picea pungens & varieties
Bournemouth Pine ...................................Pinus pinaster
Box .......................................................................Buxus
Bottle Brush..........................................Callistemon laevis
Box Elder.................................Acer negundo & varieties
Broad Leaved Lime .................................Tilia platyphyllos
Bhutan Pine..........................................Pinus wallichiana

Cabbage Tree .................................Cordyline australis
Camperdown Elm ...........................Ulmus glabra Camperdownii
Canadian Maple.................................Acer rubrum & varieties
Candyfloss Tree .................................Cercidiphyllum japonicum
Cappadoci Maple.........................Acer cappadocicum & varieties
Cedar ...........................................................Cedrus & varieties
Cedar of Lebanon ...............................................Cedrus libani
Cherry...........................................................Prunus & varieties
Chestnut Leaved Oak ...................................Quercus castaneifolia
Chinese Date ...............................................Ziziphus guiggiolo
Chinese Privet.........................Ligustrum lucidum & varieties
Chusan Palm ...........................................Trachycarpus fortunei
Coastal Redwood .....................................Sequoia sempervirens
Contorted Willow ...............................Salix matsudana Tortuosa
Common Lime.....................................Tilia europaea & varieties
Cork Oak ..................................................Quercus suber
Copper Beech.............................Fagus sylvatica Purpurea
Cornelian Cherry ........................................Cornus mas
Crab Apple..................................................Malus & varieties
Crape Myrtle .............................Lagerstroemia indica & varieties
Cypress........................................Cupressus arizonica Glauca &
Cupressus macrocarpa Goldcrest
Cypress Oak .........................Quercus robur Fastigiata & varieties

Date Plum..............................................Diospyrus lotus
Dawn Redwood.............................Metasequoia glyptostroboides
Deodar Cedar ...............................................Cedrus deodara
Desert Willow .................Chitalpa tashkentensis Summer Bells
Dogwood...........................................Cornus & varieties
Dove Tree ...........................................Davidia involucrata

Elm.........................................................Ulmus & varieties
English Oak ...............................................Quercus robur
Eucalyptus ...............................Eucalyptus & varieties

False Acacia .................................Robinia & varieties
Flowering Ash .............................Fraxinus ornus & varieties
Field Maple .............................Acer campestre & varieties
Fig.............................................................................Ficus
Fir.............................................................................Abies
Fox Glove Tree .................................Paulownia tomentosa

Giant Redwood .............................Sequoiadendron giganteum
Golden Rain .............................Laburnum & varieties
Golden Ash...........................Fraxinus excelsior Jaspidea
Gum Tree.....................................Eucalyptus & varieties

Hackberry.............................................Celtis occidentalis
Handkerchief Tree......................................Davidia & varieties
Hawthorn...........................................Crataegus & varieties
Hazel ..................................................Corylus & varieties
Holly ...........................................................Ilex & varieties
Holm Oak ...........................................Quercus ilex
Honey Locust ...............................Gleditsia & varieties
Hop Hornbeam.............................Ostrya carpinifolia
Hornbeam .............................................Carpinus & varieties
Horse Chestnut....................................Aesculus & varieties
Himalayan Birch .............................Betula utilis & varieties
Hungarian Oak ...........................................Quercus frainetto

Incense Cedar .............................Calocedrus decurrans
Indian Bean Tree .............................Catalpa & varieties
Irish Juniper..............................Juniperus communis Hibernica

Japanese Angelica Tree....................................Aralia elata
Japanese Cedar.............................................Cryptomeria
Japanese Maple .....................................Acer palmatum & varieties
Japanese Pagoda Tree..................Sophora japonica & varieties
Jelly Palm.................................................Butta capitata
Judas Tree ....................................Cercis siliquastrum & varieties
June Berry .............................Amelanchier & varieties

Katsura.............................................Cercidiphyllum japonicum
Keaki ....................................Zelkova serrata & varieties
Kentucky Coffee Tree .............................Gymnocladus dioica
Killarney Strawberry Tree......................................Arbutus unedo
Kilmarnock Willow......................................Salix caprea Pendula
Kusamaki.................................................................Podocarpus

Telephone 01353 720 748   •   www.barcham.co.uk   •   Fax 01353 723 060

| | |
|---|---|
| Larch | Larix & varieties |
| Laurel | Prunus rotundifolia / laurocerasus |
| Leyland Cypress | Cupressocyparis leylandii & varieties |
| Lime | Tilia & varieties |
| Lobels Maple | Acer lobelii |
| Lombardy Poplar | Populus nigra Italica |
| London Plane | Platanus hispanica |
| Magnolia | Magnolia & varieties |
| Maidenhair Tree | Ginkgo & varieties |
| Manna Ash | Fraxinus ornus & varieties |
| May Tree | Crataegus & varieties |
| Medlar | Mespilus germanica |
| Mongolian Lime | Tilia mongolica |
| Mountain Ash | Sorbus aucuparia & varieties |
| Monkey Puzzle | Araucaria araucana |
| Monterey Pine | Pinus radiata |
| Mulberry | Morus & varieties |
| Nettle Tree | Celtis australis |
| Norway Maple | Acer platanoides & varieties |
| Oak | Quercus & varieties |
| Olive | Olea europaeus |
| One-leaved Ash | Fraxinus excelsior Diversifolia |
| Oriental Plane | Platanus orientalis & varieties |
| Paper Birch | Betula papyrifera |
| Paper Mulberry | Broussonetia papyrifera |
| Paperbark Maple | Acer griseum |
| Pear | Pyrus & varieties |
| Pencil Cedar | Cupressus sempervirens |
| Persian Iron Wood | Parrotia persica & varieties |
| Pin Oak | Quercus palustris |
| Pine | Pinus & varieties |
| Pineapple Guava | Feijoa sellowiana |
| Plum | Prunus domestica |
| Poplar | Populus & varieties |
| Portugal Laurel | Prunus lusitanica |
| Pride of India | Koelreuteria paniculata & varieties |
| Privet | Ligustrum & varieties |
| Purple Leaf Plum | Prunus cerasifera Nigra |
| Pussy Willow | Salix caprea |
| Redbud | Cercis & varieties |
| Red Maple | Acer rubrum & varieties & Acer freemanii Autumn Blaze |
| Red Twigged Lime | Tilia platyphyllos Rubra |
| Red Oak | Quercus rubra |
| Redwood | Sequoia |
| River Birch | Betula nigra |
| Rose of Sharon | Hibiscus |
| Rowan | Sorbus aucuparia & varieties |

| | |
|---|---|
| Scarlet Oak | Quercus coccinea |
| Scarlet Willow | Salix alba Chermesina |
| Scots Pine | Pinus sylvestris |
| Sentinel Pine | Pinus sylvestris Fastigiata |
| Serbian Spruce | Picea omorika |
| Serviceberry | Amelanchier & varieties |
| Sessile Oak | Quercus petraea |
| Shingle Oak | Quercus imbricaria |
| Silver Birch | Betula pendula & varieties |
| Silver Maple | Acer saccharinum & varieties |
| Silver Lime | Tilia tomentosa & varieties |
| Silver Wattle | Acacia dealbata |
| Small Leaved Lime | Tilia cordata & varieties |
| Swedish Birch | Betula Dalecarlica |
| Swedish Upright | Populus tremula Erecta |
| Sweet Gum | Liquidambar & varieties |
| Snakebark Maple | Acer |
| Snowy Mespilus | Amelanchier & varieties |
| Stone Pine | Pinus pinea |
| Sumach | Rhus typhina |
| Swamp Cypress | Taxodium distichum |
| Swedish Whitebeam | Sorbus intermedia & varieties |
| Sweet Chestnut | Castanea sativa & varieties |
| Sweet Gum | Liquidambar & varieties |
| Swiss Mountain Pine | Pinus mugo |
| Sycamore | Acer pseudoplatanus & varieties |
| Thorn | Crataegus & varieties |
| Tree of Heaven | Ailanthus altissima |
| Trident Maple | Acer buergerianum |
| Tulip Tree | Liriodendron tulipifera |
| Turkish Hazel | Corylus colurna |
| Turkey Oak | Quercus cerris |
| Violet Willow | Salix daphnoides |
| Walnut | Juglans & varieties |
| Wedding Cake Tree | Cornus controversa |
| Weeping Birch | Betula pendula Tristis & Youngii |
| Weeping Willow | Salix alba Tristis (Chrysocoma) |
| Whitebeam | Sorbus aria & varieties |
| Witch Hazel | Hamamelis |
| White Willow | Salix alba |
| Wild Cherry | Prunus avium & varieties |
| Wild Service Tree | Sorbus torminalis |
| Willow | Salix & varieties |
| Wing Nut | Pterocarya fraxinifolia |
| Western West Cedar | Thujia plicata & varieties |
| Yew | Taxus baccata |

# The value of trees

We derive so much enjoyment from trees yet the amount they contribute to our existence is often overlooked. Their role as a backdrop is accepted but never actively considered other than by enthusiasts who are aware of their benefits already.

The media create a constant steam of unsettling stories about climate change with its likely impact on current generations and on the generations to come. Trees absorb carbon dioxide, one of the principle greenhouse gases. Trees provide shelter and shade and it has been estimated that they can save up to 10% of the energy needed to heat or cool nearby buildings. Trees slow down the rate at which rainwater hits the ground and bind soils to stabilize embankments, which helps to reduce the likelihood of flash flooding and soil erosion. Trees are sustainable, plastic isn't.

Health is something each and every one of us strives for. Trees filter out atmospheric pollutants. Trees shade out harmful solar radiation and have a positive effect on the incidence of asthma. Trees can assist in the cleaning up of contaminated land.

Property owners share a common interest in the value of their assets. Trees, it has been estimated, can increase property values by as much as 18%, with houses and homes in tree lined avenues much desired and sought after. Ask any estate agent. Trees also mask the intrusive nature of many developments where space is at a premium.

Many of the every day products we buy from supermarkets and garden centres originate from trees. Trees yield fruit and nuts. Trees provide horticultural mulch. Trees yield timber for construction and furniture. Renewable fossil fuel, high value chemicals and pharmaceuticals may be the wood products of the future.

Ecosystems and ecological niches have become buzz words of our times. Trees provide valuable environmental habitats for a myriad of creatures both large and small. Trees bring the countryside into town. Trees enhance the character of local areas. Trees soften the landscape of hard edged towns, making them greener and more attractive. Many government advisory notes emphasise the importance of sustainable communities. Trees contribute to the landscape where people meet. Community involvement in woodland creation and maintenance is on the increase with people becoming more aware and involved in their local environment.

Archaeology is associated with digs, fossils and ruins. Yet trees provide an everyday link with both the past and the future. Ancient woodlands provide a link with craft, woodland management skills, and life styles now almost forgotten. Trees offer many clues to a historic past which can be seen for those who wish to look. Trees provide long lived memorials to those no longer with us.

A salutary thought, many of the most significant trees in our towns and cities were planted more than a century ago, providing a living legacy for everyone to enjoy and benefit from today. How many of us remember being told as a youngster that planting a tree was the most unselfish thing one could ever do?

# ABIES grandis
*Giant Fir*

Native to North America where it can grow up to 75 metres in height, this fast growing conifer was introduced by David Douglas in 1830. It grows best on well drained soils, is lime tolerant, and thrives in areas with high annual rainfall so is mostly seen in the north and west of the UK.

The fragrant leaves, which can be 3-6cm long, are characterised by two grey-blue bands underneath. Cones are produced up to 10cm in length and are vivid green when young. The largest UK example was planted at Stone, Argyll, in 1876 and had reached over 63 metres tall a hundred years later.

Mature height: 20m+ | Shape of mature tree | Evergreen trees

# ABIES koreana
*Korean Fir*

**Introduced in 1905 from Korea, this slow growing fir forms a stout compact tree at maturity and is characterised by its violet / purple cylindrical cones that can get to 7cm in length.**

It is tolerant of more heat than most firs but still thrives best in colder climates. The 1-2cm leaves are dark green above and white beneath divided by a thin green midrib. Remarkably, the glorious cone display is prominent even on young trees that are only 1-2 metres in height.

Mature height: 10-15m | Shape of mature tree | Evergreen trees

# ABIES nordmanniana
*Nordmann/Caucasian Fir*

Introduced from Northern Turkey in 1840, this striking conifer has risen steeply in popularity over recent years for being a 'needle fast' Christmas tree. Arguably the most attractive of the firs it can grow immensely tall with some specimens in Europe attaining 85m in height.

**Its tiered branches support dark green leaves 2-3cm in length with cones that can grow up to 20cm. It is very robust and disease resistant but our advice is to plant after the 25th December for municipal plantings! Like most firs it tends to scorch up in very hot climates but is well suited for growing in the UK.**

Mature height: 20m+ | Shape of mature tree | Evergreen trees

# ACACIA dealbata
## *Silver Wattle*

This fast growing pioneer species is a native of Southern Australia and Tasmania and was introduced to the UK in 1820 but is only hardy down to about -5 Celsius.

The evergreen greenish blue leaves are bipinnate and the trees are overtaken by profuse racemes of fragrant bright yellow flowers in spring. We recommend this tree to be planted in protected south facing aspects in Southern England as until they girth up they can be susceptible to getting nipped back by frost. Until the bark matures the trunk is a smooth blue which adds to its exotic appeal.

Mature height: 5-10m    Shape of mature tree    Flowering trees

# ACER buergerianum
## *Trident Maple*

**Native to Eastern China and Korea, this very pretty maple was introduced in 1890. It forms an oval to rounded crown at maturity and is well suited to streets or gardens.**

New spring foliage emerges a rich bronze colour before hardening to a glossy dark green by summer. Greenish yellow flowers are borne in March and maturing trunks flake to brown / orange colours to provide a patchwork of winter interest. Autumn colours can be variable but seldom disappointing with leaves turning yellow through to red before falling. It is considered a slow to medium grower and is fully hardy down to -25 Celsius.

Mature height: 10-15m    Shape of mature tree    Urban trees

Recent arborist opinion coming out of the USA place this as a highly prized urban tree. Its increased popularity is not only due to its seasonal interest but also its durability. For the UK it represents an alternative to Acer campestre types.

# ACER campestre
## *Field Maple*

Native to England, but not in Scotland or Ireland, this small to medium tree of rounded form was widely used in the Middle Ages for making musical instruments. In autumn its leaves turn not just clear yellow, but also red and golden brown.

It does best in rich, well drained soils, but is equally at home in virtually any soil type, and will readily tolerate drought, soil compaction and air pollution. A versatile, resilient and attractive species with a wide range of uses. Available both as multi-stem and single stem.

Mature height: 10-15m+

Shape of mature tree

Multi-stem

Native trees

Field Maple also makes an excellent hedgerow plant. Being native, it is very 'wildlife friendly' and it can cope well to rough pruning during the dormant season to keep the hedge to shape. Many of its clones listed next are far more suitable for urban and street planting as they form crowns of more regular shape than that of their parent.

# ACER campestre Arends

**This cultivar of Field Maple has a much more regular and oval habit than the species. We were first introduced to it in the mid 1990s and placed it into our range soon after as its habit ticked all the boxes for urban planting.**

It does best in rich, well drained soils, but does well in virtually any soil type, and will readily tolerate drought, soil compaction and air pollution. Compared to Norway Maple types, Acer campestre clones have much smaller leaves so are a better prospect in the urban environment at leaf fall.

Mature height: 10-15m

Shape of mature tree

Urban trees

# ACER campestre Elegant

This cultivar of Field Maple is, in our opinion, the pick of the Acer campestre clones for street planting. It retains a compact ascending habit, is vigorous in growth, and gives uniformity if planted in an avenue. Many clones are tricky to tell apart at maturity but Elegant's stubby thick growth makes it easier to distinguish.

It does best in rich, well drained soils, but does well in virtually any soil type, and will readily tolerate drought, soil compaction and air pollution. Typical of its type, it can go a glorious yellow in autumn and is a great host to a range of native wildlife.

Mature height: 10-15m    Shape of mature tree    Urban trees

# ACER campestre Elsrijk

This cultivar of the Field Maple is named after the park in Amstelveen, Holland, where it was discovered in the 1950s. It differs from the species in that it has a more regular, oval habit. At maturity one could mistake it for straight forward Acer campestre but one with a lovely compact shape.

**It does best in rich, well drained soils, but does well in virtually any soil type, and will readily tolerate drought, soil compaction and air pollution. A medium sized tree which we particularly recommend for urban and street plantings, its foliage turns a magnificent clear yellow in autumn.**

Mature height: 10-15m    Shape of mature tree    Urban trees

Telephone 01353 720 748   •   www.barcham.co.uk   •   Fax 01353 723 060

# ACER campestre Louisa Red Shine

A most attractive small to medium tree with a rounded habit. The new leaves are flushed with crimson before turning mauve / green as the season progresses. There are very few trees with native origin that have this degree of leaf colour and as it has smaller leaves than the red clones of Norway Maple it provides softer contrast on the landscape.

It does best in rich, well drained soils, but does well in virtually any soil type, and will readily tolerate drought, soil compaction and air pollution. An ideal subject for streets, parks and verges, it has been used with great effect in London in recent years. Each growth flush is rewarded with red to crimson leaves so there is plenty of interest throughout the summer.

**10|15**
Mature height: 10-15m

Shape of mature tree

Urban trees

The foliage display turns to yellow with hints of orange by the autumn to round off eight months of succession leaf interest. Being of native origin it is also a good host to insects and birds.

## ACER campestre Nanum

**A top worked variety with a very dwarfing, rounded habit. Its leaves are smaller than those of the species and they form a very dense crown.**

It does best in rich, well drained soils, but does well in virtually any soil type, and will readily tolerate drought, soil compaction and air pollution. Very good for streets and residential plantings, or any site where space is at a premium. This clone has long been in cultivation and was introduced in the 1830s.

Mature height: 5m | Shape of mature tree | Urban trees

## ACER campestre Queen Elizabeth

This American cultivar is also known as Evelyn and was introduced in the mid 1980s. It is fast growing, has a relatively narrow habit and is larger and darker leaved than the species. The ascending branches are produced at angle of 45° to the dominant central leader.

It does best in rich, well drained soils, but does well in virtually any soil type, and will readily tolerate drought, soil compaction and air pollution. An excellent choice as a street tree, it has a tighter habit than Elsrijk and was first brought into general cultivation by the well known Frank Schmidt nursery in Oregon.

Mature height: 10-15m | Shape of mature tree | Urban trees

● Telephone 01353 720 748   ● www.barcham.co.uk   ● Fax 01353 723 060

Barcham

# ACER cappadocicum

This broad spreading maple has five to seven-lobed green glossy leaves that turn a glorious yellow in autumn. The bark is veined with a hint of yellow when young and it is a native of Western Asia to Himalaya.

Tip die back is commonly seen on these genera during establishment, sometimes causing a complete collapse of the plant, and this is generally caused by verticillium. This fungus accounts for many in the maple family and is carried on water so is difficult to avoid. Like Acer rubrum, the susceptibility is probably caused by inadequate availability of trace elements such as manganese.

15|20
Mature height:
15-20m

Shape of
mature tree

Autumn
colour

# ACER cappadocicum Aureum

A smaller tree than its parent, Acer cappadocicum, this attractive tree flushes a bright yellow in the spring and retains this splendour through to the autumn. It prefers sheltered conditions and is not tolerant to urban pollution.

**It is particularly effective when planted against an evergreen backdrop as the foliage provides a vivid contrast. Best planted on sites offering good light levels but not in areas with reflected light bouncing off hard surfaces.**

10|15
Mature height:
10-15m

Shape of
mature tree

Yellow
foliage

This tree is difficult to grow and establish but the rewards are great if you succeed. It is rarely seen at maturity in the UK and if you are in doubt about its suitability to your planting scheme but still want a yellow foliaged maple, consider using Acer platanoides Princeton Gold or Acer pseudoplatanus Worleii and Corstorphinense as tougher, but just as pretty, alternatives.

# ACER cappadocicum Rubrum

Also known as the Caucasian Maple, this cultivar dates back to at least 1838 but remains rather uncommon. It is a medium to large tree with a rounded habit. The young, dark red leaves turn green and then back to red, gold and yellow in autumn. This superb autumn colour lasts for many weeks.

Although best on moist, well drained soil, it is adaptable and flourishes in either full sun or light shade. It is best grown with a little shelter from strong winds. A good tree for avenues and verges, but not good where soil becomes compacted.

Mature height: 15-20m+

Shape of mature tree

Autumn colour

# ACER x freemanii Armstrong

Selected by Newton Armstrong in the States in 1947, this small to medium tree has a tightly columnar habit, making it very useful as a street and car park tree. It is half Acer rubrum and half Acer saccharinum but the latter dominates with autumn colour of orange and yellows rather than glorious scarlet.

The toughness of its Silver Maple parentage makes it a better bet than Acer rubrum and its cultivars when manganese is not present in the soil. It tolerates urban conditions but as a warning note is very susceptible to glyphosate (Roundup) so beware.

Mature height: 10-15m

Shape of mature tree

Autumn Colour

● Telephone 01353 720 748 ● www.barcham.co.uk ● Fax 01353 723 060

Barcham

# ACER x freemanii Autumn Blaze

This is a cultivar of a naturally occurring hybrid of Acer rubrum and Acer saccharinum, named after Oliver Freeman, who made the crossing at the US National Arboretum in the 1930s.

**This vigorous, oval headed, large tree has dark green, deeply indented leaves, which turn rich flame red in autumn. Acer rubrum is often specified for this effect but very rarely does well on UK soils as it is dependent on the trace element manganese which it can only access at low ph. Autumn Blaze possesses the prettiness of rubrum but the toughness of saccharinum so it is the much safer bet.**

Mature height:
20m+

Shape of
mature tree

Autumn
colour

This variety is very highly thought of in the United States where there are nurseries, principally in Oregon, that grow little else to satisfy their domestic market. It is a highly dramatic tree, rivalling even Liquidambar for autumn colour. As a word of caution, it is slightly brittle, so planting sites exposed to strong and persistent winds should be avoided.

# ACER ginnala
*Amur Maple*

Its common name derives from the Amur River, which divides China and Russia. One of the very best trees for autumn colour, when its foliage turns a stunning red, it is also very early into leaf in spring and produces yellow-white fragrant flowers in May. This is a small to medium tree with a rounded habit, and is good for parks and public gardens.

It flourishes in full sun or light shade and in most soil types, and has the added advantages of being wind and drought resistant.

Mature height:
10-15m

Shape of
mature tree

Autumn
Colour

# ACER griseum
## *Paperbark Maple*

A small tree, but a magnificent one! Originally from China, from an early age the bark peels to reveal cinnamon coloured under-bark and the trifoliate leaves have attractive reddish tints in autumn. Introduced by Ernest Wilson in 1901.

This maple does well in sun or partial shade and appreciates a sheltered position. Growing tips generally frost out over winter giving the tree a very rounded habit. It does best in moist, well drained soil, and is not drought tolerant. Nutrient rich, wet soil can inhibit autumn colour.

Mature height: 5-10m   Shape of mature tree   Bark interest

It is always tempting to plant a tree as pleasing as this in a hard area subjected to reflected heat and light but in view for all to see. It is so important to match the tree's physiology with complementing planting locations for the plant to thrive. This tree will fare poorly when surrounded by hard surfaces.

# ACER lobelii
## *Lobels Maple*

**Thought to be a naturally occurring hybrid between Acer platanoides and Acer cappadocicum, this native of Southern Italy was introduced in 1683 and is one of the few maples to be naturally fastigiate.**

Great for restricted spaces, this vigorous narrow growing maple tolerates most soils and turns a glorious yellow in the autumn. Dark green leaves in summer gives the tree a very neat and tidy appearance and its juvenile smooth grey bark graduates to a browner and shallowly furrowed trunk at maturity.

Mature height: 10-15m   Shape of mature tree   Narrow trees

Telephone 01353 720 748   www.barcham.co.uk   Fax 01353 723 060

# ACER negundo
## *Box Elder*

A medium to large tree, which is particularly fast growing in its first few years. A row of these makes a good screen or windbreak, and it is well worth considering where there is an incidence of honey fungus as it shows good resistance. Its compound leaves, more like those of an ash, make this species unique among maples.

A good choice for heavy clay soils and for waterside plantings, it performs just as well in lighter, drier ones. It also tolerates air pollution and soil compaction as well as withstanding periodic flooding. Native of the USA, this tree is a real tough performer.

Mature height: 15-20m

Shape of mature tree

Clay soils

# ACER negundo Flamingo

This male clone, raised in Holland in the 1970s, has young leaves that have a wide, soft pink margin which turns to white. Best displays of foliage appear when plants are hard pruned in winter. We supply bottom worked standard trees as it tends to break out when top worked onto a negundo stem.

**A good choice for heavy clay soils and for waterside plantings, it performs just as well in lighter, drier ones. It also tolerates air pollution and soil compaction. Very adaptable and recommended as a garden or verge tree.**

Mature height: 10-15m

Shape of mature tree

Variegated trees

# ACER palmatum
## *Japanese Maple*

The Japanese maple was introduced from its native land to Britain in the 1820s. Also a native of both China and Korea, this magnificent tree can outstrip size expectation if left alone in an area large enough to accommodate.

A delightful, small tree for a sheltered position such as a courtyard or an urban garden. It has a rounded habit and its deeply lobed leaves turn shades of yellow, red and orange in autumn. They do best in rich, moist, but free draining, loamy soils. It is remarkably self reliant post establishment for seemingly such a dainty tree.

| 5\|10 | | |
|---|---|---|
| Mature height: 5-10m | Shape of mature tree | Garden trees |

# ACER palmatum Bloodgood

A superb Japanese maple with long lasting and unfading reddish purple leaves that turn a glorious red before they drop in autumn. This clone won the Award of Garden Merit in 2002.

Recognised as one of the best clones of its type, it also produces beautiful red fruits and is particularly hardy even in the coldest of winters. We grow this as a full standard tree with a rounded crown so it is best suited for gardens and parks. It thrives on most soils.

| 5\|10 | | |
|---|---|---|
| Mature height: 5-10m | Shape of mature tree | Red/purple foliage |

# ACER palmatum Dissectum Garnet

**A lovely cut leaf deep purple Japanese maple that was raised in Holland around 1950 and won the Award of Garden Merit in 2002.**

It is a strong growing form with good autumn colour. We grow this as a full standard tree with a rounded crown so it is best suited for gardens and parks. It thrives on most soils. When grown under the shade of other trees the leaves are more dark green than purple so make sure it has plenty of light to trigger the true colour of the summer foliage display.

| 5\|10 | | |
|---|---|---|
| Mature height: 5-10m | Shape of mature tree | Red/purple foliage |

● Telephone 01353 720 748   ● www.barcham.co.uk   ● Fax 01353 723 060

# ACER palmatum Fireglow

Developed around 1977, this is thought to be an improved clone of the superb 'Bloodgood'. In truth there is little to choose between them so try not to agonise over the choice!

We grow this as a full standard tree with a rounded crown so it is best suited for gardens and parks. It thrives on most soils. The glorious display of summer leaves provide great contrast in any garden so time should be taken to carefully select its planting position to achieve greatest effect. As a rule the eye picks up on deep reds and purples first, if you place it further back in your landscape it draws the focus through your garden rather than blocking off the view behind it.

Mature height: 5-10m | Shape of mature tree | Red/purple foliage

# ACER palmatum Lionheart

**When you have been in arboriculture for as long as I have it is a delight to get introduced to a fine plant like 'Lionheart'. I am now the proud owner of one that sits beautifully in my garden!**

We grow this clone as a quarter standard as it's finely dissected leaves give such a lovely soft contrast to a border or patio display when viewed from above. The leaf colour is tricky to describe as it has hints of dark green, red, burgundy and purple but the overall effect is very pleasing! Autumn colour is similarly striking. Ideal for a small garden border or on a patio in a contrasting planter that is large enough to give the plant longevity.

Mature height: 1-3m | Shape of mature tree | Red/purple foliage

# ACER palmatum Osakazuki

The best of all Japanese Maples for red autumn colour, this clone won the Award of Garden Merit in 2002 and was introduced in the 1880s.

An attractive, small tree for a sheltered position such as a courtyard or an urban garden. It has a rounded habit and its deeply lobed leaves turn shades of yellow, red and orange in autumn. They do best in rich, moist, but free draining, loamy soils. A stunning tree that never fails to impress.

Mature height: 5-10m | Shape of mature tree | Autumn colour

# ACER palmatum Purpurea

**A superb tree for those who like purple foliage, this clone was introduced in the 1850s but has since been unfairly superseded by improved selections such as Bloodgood.**

It makes a small tree for a sheltered position such as a courtyard or an urban garden and has a rounded habit with its deeply lobed purple leaves turning shades of luminescent red in autumn.

They do best in rich, moist, but free draining, loamy soils.

| 5\|10 | | |
|---|---|---|
| Mature height: 5-10m | Shape of mature tree | Red/purple foliage |

# ACER platanoides
*Norway Maple*

An imposing and fast growing tree of great size and the parent of the many cultivars listed on the following pages. The yellow flowers appear in spring, ahead of the leaves which turn yellow and sometimes red in autumn.

A native tree of Norway and Europe, but not of Britain, and used widely in parks and streets.

Many of its cultivars are more suitable for urban and street planting as they form crowns of more regular shape than that of their parent.

### Norway Maple

It does well on most soil types, tolerates air pollution and resists drought. Its clonal selections are generally preferred as seedling plants can grow to large proportions and create maintenance issues in streets and urban corridors.

| 20+ | | |
|---|---|---|
| Mature height: 20m+ | Shape of mature tree | Urban trees |

Telephone 01353 720 748 • www.barcham.co.uk • Fax 01353 723 060

# ACER platanoides Cleveland

In cultivation since 1948, this selection has an upright habit and an oval head of branches with big, dark green foliage. Very good as a street tree and for urban plantings.

Considered as one of the best clones for street planting by arborists in America, it does well on most soil types, tolerates air pollution and resists drought. It has an excellent autumn colour of golden yellow and retains its oval to rounded habit through to maturity.

 **15|20**
Mature height: 15-20m

 Shape of mature tree

 Urban trees

# ACER platanoides Columnare

Raised in France by Simon–Louis nursery in the 1850s, this slow growing cultivar has an oval / compact habit and is superb as a street tree because its columnar form needs virtually no maintenance. The crown stays closed even when the tree is mature.

It does well on most soil types, tolerates air pollution and resists drought. The Dutch have confused matters by calling several similar types 'Columnare' but we reckon they are all distinctly different so beware!! From Barcham you will get the original and what we think is the best clone.

 **5|10**
Mature height: 5-10m

 Shape of mature tree

 Urban trees

# ACER platanoides
# Crimson King

A large and most impressive tree with a well rounded form, it looks good from spring through to autumn as its red foliage turns gradually to maroon. A seedling of Schwedleri, it was raised in Belgium in the 1930s.

It does well on most soil types, tolerates air pollution and resists drought. The yellow flowers contrast impressively against the dark emerging spring foliage. We so often see this tree planted in avenues too close together but there is no need as it is quick to grow. Ten metres should be the minimum planting distance but planting in bulk can give too much of a good thing in that the dark leaves tends to gobble up all the light and create a sombre environment below.

A tougher and quicker prospect than Purple Beech, this can be planted on the boundary of a site to draw the eye through the landscape. Dark leaved trees can be superb for defining the overall effect of the landscape but only if used sparingly. Too often I see this tree planted in areas where it will have to be felled before maturity as the planting position is too small to accommodate it.

20+
Mature height:
20m+

Shape of
mature tree

Red/purple
foliage

● Telephone 01353 720 748  ● www.barcham.co.uk  ● Fax 01353 723 060

Barcham

# ACER platanoides
# Deborah

Another seedling from Schwedleri, fast growing Deborah comes from Canada and makes a large tree with a rounded form. Introduced in the 1970s, the spring leaves are bright red, gradually turning to dark green. When the second flush appears there is a superb contrast between the red and the green foliage together.

It does well on most soil types, tolerates air pollution and resists drought. The leaves have a distinctive wavy margin and colour to a rich orange / yellow in the autumn. Most suitable for parks, verges and large gardens.

Its newly emerging flush of spring red leaves are particularly effective against the profuse yellow flowers that are borne in April. For those of you who feel 'Royal Red' or 'Crimson King' are too much, 'Deborah' offers a superb compromise

15|20
Mature height:
15-20m

Shape of
mature tree

Urban
trees

# ACER platanoides Drummondii

In cultivation since 1903, this form produces magnificently variegated foliage which has a wide, creamy white margin. It is widely known in North America as the Harlequin Maple. Any shoots which show signs of reversion are best removed. A medium to large tree with a rounded form.

**It does well on most soil types, tolerates air pollution and resists drought. It is most impressive in the spring when the variegation is at its most vivid but summer winds can bruise the leaf margins of young trees which then scorch brown. This however is only superficial and does not affect its performance the following year.**

This clone can provide vivid contrast within a garden, particularly against a dark evergreen backdrop so take care to place this tree as the results can be very rewarding. It won the Award of Merit in 1956.

10|15

Mature height: 10-15m

Shape of mature tree

Variegated trees

● Telephone 01353 720 748  ● www.barcham.co.uk  ● Fax 01353 723 060

# ACER platanoides
# Emerald Queen

Selected in the USA in the late 1950s, this has a brighter green leaf colour and more regular habit than the species. It tends to keep a dominant central leader and a more regular habit. A superb cultivar and strongly recommended for street and urban plantings. Where uniformity is required, this is a far better choice than its parent, Acer platanoides.

| 10\|15 | | |
|---|---|---|
| Mature height: 10-15m+ | Shape of mature tree | Urban trees |

It does well on most soil types, tolerates air pollution and resists drought. Although ascending when young, it usually gets as wide as it gets broad after about 25 years so it is only ideal for wide verges and areas large enough to accommodate it. It is by far the most popular of the Norway Maple clones and a much safer bet than planting the seedling parent.

# ACER platanoides Fairview

**This tough newcomer to our range is derived from a seedling of 'Crimson King'. It thrives on poor urban soils and maintains an upright oval habit and at maturity its dimensions are approximately 15 metres tall with a diameter of 12 metres, making it a very useful urban tree.**

Reddish purple foliage in the spring hardens to a deep bronze by late summer. It bears green / yellow flowers from April onwards that are a lovely contrast with the dark leaves as they first emerge. This is the narrowest upright dark leaved Norway Maple we stock. We have often been tempted by Acer platanoides Crimson Sentry but this is so often plagued by mildew that it is not worth the trouble.

| 10\|15 | | |
|---|---|---|
| Mature height: 10-15m | Shape of mature tree | Urban trees |

# ACER platanoides Farlakes Green

This Swedish clone has similar characteristics to those of Emerald Queen, but does not grow quite as high. This clone is preferred in Scandinavia as it is deemed hardier, resisting very low temperatures.

It does well on most soil types, tolerates air pollution and resists drought. Yellow spring flowers are replaced by crisp green foliage that turns yellow in autumn. A better clone for exposed conditions, we would recommend it more the further north you get.

| 10\|15 | | |
|---|---|---|
| Mature height: 10-15m+ | Shape of mature tree | Urban trees |

# ACER platanoides Globosum

**Introduced in the early 1870s, this 'lollipop' tree is top grafted onto platanoides stem to form a dense mop headed tree. A very good choice as a street tree and for urban plantings and particularly popular in Germany.**

It does well on most soil types, tolerates air pollution and resists drought. The dense rounded formality of the crown makes this a delight for architects seeking contrast. Wonderful when in full foliage, it can be rather a let down in a garden after leaf fall as the crown network is small and stubby. Best for urban environments where small is beautiful.

| 5\|10 | | |
|---|---|---|
| Mature height: 5-10m | Shape of mature tree | Urban trees |

# ACER platanoides Olmstead

Selected in Rochester, New York, in the mid 1950s, this cultivar is similar to Acer platanoides Columnare in having a columnar habit. A good choice as a street tree and where space is restricted.

It does well on most soil types, tolerates air pollution and resists drought. Generally at maturity its height is twice its breadth making this a popular urban tree requiring little maintenance.

| 10\|15 | | |
|---|---|---|
| Mature height: 10-15m | Shape of mature tree | Urban trees |

● Telephone 01353 720 748   ● www.barcham.co.uk   ● Fax 01353 723 060

# ACER platanoides Princeton Gold

Also known as Prigo, this sparkling new cultivar has golden yellow spring foliage which hardens to yellow / green in summer. We recommend it for both park and street planting.

Developed in the States, the foliage can tend to scorch up in really hot conditions so it is not widely used. However, our wonderfully temperate climate in the UK suits it down to the ground and the leaf colour makes it one of the best 'yellows' on the market. It does well on most soil types, tolerates air pollution and resists drought.

 10|15 Mature height: 10-15m

 Shape of mature tree

 Yellow foliage

There are very few reliable yellow foliaged trees that thrive in the UK but in our opinion this clone rates as one that shouldn't be overlooked. Lighter coloured leaves can provide stunning contrast to a garden with a sombre evergreen backdrop.

# ACER platanoides
# Royal Red

A large tree with a crown which is originally conical before becoming broadly round. It has dark purple leaves which turn golden yellow and orange in autumn. Attractive, bright red "keys" are an added feature. Yellow flowers in spring contrast beautifully with emerging purple foliage.

**Supposedly smaller and hardier than 'Crimson King' there is an underlying suspicion that it is in fact the same tree but with a different name. I can't make my mind up either way but I certainly wouldn't agonise over the choice for planting. It does well on most soil types, tolerates air pollution and resists drought.**

| 20+ | | |
|---|---|---|
| Mature height: 20m+ | Shape of mature tree | Red/purple foliage |

● Telephone 01353 720 748 ● www.barcham.co.uk ● Fax 01353 723 060

# ACER pseudoplatanus
## *Sycamore*

A native of central and southern Europe, the Sycamore has long been naturalised in Britain. Its wood has been used for making innumerable small items from violins to wooden spoons. It is a very large tree, and very fast growing for the first 20 years. It is also one of the very toughest. Many of its cultivars are smaller, but equally as durable.

It tolerates air pollution and thrives in most soils, and is particularly useful for coastal sites where it can make an effective defence against strong winds and salt-laden air. Interestingly, recent work is now suggesting Sycamore is actually a native tree of the UK with both pollen and wood samples predating historical measures.

## *Sycamore*

Native or not the environmental impact of common Sycamore should not be understated. It makes a wonderful host to a wide range of our wildlife and provides a refuge in landscapes that do not readily support any other species.

The success of this tree gives it an unfair tag of being rather a 'weed'. It is however an incredibly versatile plant that thrives in the most difficult of circumstances so it shouldn't be overlooked. Improved clones such as 'Negenia' are widely used on the continent as a street / verge tree as it forms a more regular crown shape at maturity.

20+
Mature height 20m+

Shape of mature tree

Coastal sites

## ACER pseudoplatanus Brilliantissimum

Smaller than the species and much slower growing, this top worked cultivar forms a round and dense crown. The young leaves in spring are a wonderful shell pink, hardening to light green by June. An excellent street tree and for where space is limited.

It tolerates air pollution and thrives in most soils, and is particularly useful for coastal sites where it can make an effective defence against strong winds and salt-laden air. Introduced in the early 1900s, this eye catching cultivar won the Award of Garden Merit in 2002.

5|10
Mature height: 5-10m

Shape of mature tree

Garden trees

## ACER pseudoplatanus Corstorphinense

*Corstophine Plane*

It was under this tree that Lord Forrester was murdered by his sister-in-law with his own sword at Corstophine, Edinburgh, in 1679. She was then executed for the crime and it is said that the original tree is still haunted by their ghosts! The leaves are golden yellow when young, hardening to a yellow / green in summer. It is a small tree with a rounded habit that has the usual durability associated with its seedling parent.

10|15
Mature height: 10-15m

Shape of mature tree

Yellow foliage

# ACER pseudoplatanus Erectum

**Introduced around 1949, this tough and vigorous sycamore cultivar has ascending branches when young, broadening with age.**

As with many clonal selections, one would look at the form of this variety 10 years after planting and think it was just a very uniform and good selection of seedling sycamore. It tolerates air pollution and thrives in most soils, and is particularly useful for coastal sites where it can make an effective defence against strong winds and salt-laden air.

Mature height: 20m+ | Shape of mature tree | Clay soils

# ACER pseudoplatanus Leopoldii

A really eye-catching cultivar first grown in the 1860s, it is a medium tree with a rounded habit. The leaves begin yellowish pink, turning green later and are splashed with yellow and pink. Particularly attractive from leaf emergence in the spring to early summer.

It tolerates air pollution and thrives in most soils, and is particularly useful for coastal sites where it can make an effective defence against strong winds and salt-laden air. A great tree for providing contrast, it is not prone to the problem of reverting back to green like Acer platanoides Drummondii.

Mature height: 15-20m | Shape of mature tree | Variegated trees

# ACER pseudoplatanus Negenia

A vigorous, large and conical cultivar, it was selected in the late 1940s in the Netherlands, where it is widely used as a street tree. Negenia has dark green, red stalked leaves.

It tolerates air pollution and thrives in most soils, and is particularly useful for coastal sites where it can make an effective defence against strong winds and salt-laden air. Like many clones, as it matures it represents a model shape and form of its seedling parent.

Mature height: 20m+ | Shape of mature tree | Coastal sites

# ACER pseudoplatanus Spaethii

Also known as Acer pseudoplatanus Purpureum Spaethii and Acer pseudoplatanus Atropurpureum, this large tree is effective in exposed, windy sites as the underside of its foliage is purple. Introduced in the early 1860s.

It tolerates air pollution and thrives in most soils, and is particularly useful for coastal sites where it can make an effective defence against strong winds and salt-laden air.

Mature height: 15-20m | Shape of mature tree | Red/purple foliage

There are very few varieties of tree that offer an alternative leaf colour to green that can still be planted near the coast. As sea breezes are always a factor in these settings the contrast between the top and bottom sides of the leaves is constantly on display. Autumn colour is also quite dramatic so one gets an ornamental quality that can lift a drab landscape for difficult and exposed sites.

Telephone 01353 720 748 • www.barcham.co.uk • Fax 01353 723 060

# ACER pseudoplatanus Worleii
## *Golden Sycamore*

Bred in Germany in the 1890s, this is a beautiful cultivar similar to Corstorphinense. The leaves are primrose yellow as they open, darkening to gold before turning green in summer. A most elegant, medium tree.

It tolerates air pollution and thrives in most soils, and is particularly useful for coastal sites where it can make an effective defence against strong winds and salt-laden air.

Mature height: 15-20m

Shape of mature tree

Yellow foliage

Michael Dirr, the famous American arborist, has come across eight different spellings of Worleii. This represents a trait of tree growers, never satisfied until they have completely baffled their customers!

# ACER rubrum
## *Canadian Maple*

**Cultivated in Europe for its fabulous autumn colour and in America for the manufacture of furniture, this large tree has a rounded habit. The dark green leaves, slightly purple underneath, turn a brilliant scarlet in autumn.**

It tolerates air pollution and wet soil. However, as a warning note, for all the attributes of this tree it is very rarely seen thriving in the UK as it is dependent on accessing the trace element manganese which it can only derive from acid soils. Please refer back to Acer freemanii types if you haven't the soil to support your choice.

Mature height: 20m+

Shape of mature tree

Autumn Colour

# ACER rubrum Red Sunset

An American form of Red Maple, bred in the 1960s, is also known by the name "Franksred". Rated very highly by arborists for its good branch angle formation and landscape architects for its outstanding and long lived autumn display of leaf colour.

**Surely one of the most beautiful cultivars of Acer rubrum, this medium, broadly oval tree is regularly branched, and is an excellent choice for sheltered avenues. Its thick, dark, shiny foliage puts on a great display of red autumn colour. As a cautionary note, the presence of manganese in the soil is vital for Acer rubrum types to perform. Please refer back to Acer freemanii types if you haven't the soil to support your choice.**

 10|15
Mature height: 10-15m

 Shape of mature tree

 Autumn colour

# ACER rubrum Scanlon

Introduced in 1948 from the USA, this broadly columnar medium sized tree has golden leaves speckled with crimson in the autumn months. Denser than Acer freemanii Armstrong, this very worthy clone has been superseded by cultivars such as Red Sunset but still remains a good option. It has good apical dominance, retaining its leader though to maturity.

As a cautionary note, the presence of manganese in the soil is vital for Acer rubrum types to perform. Please refer back to Acer freemanii types if you haven't the soil to support your choice.

 15|20
Mature height: 15-20m

 Shape of mature tree

 Autumn colour

● Telephone 01353 720 748  ● www.barcham.co.uk  ● Fax 01353 723 060

# ACER saccharinum
## *Silver Maple*

A stately tree which grows along river banks in its native eastern North America, its common name is on account of the silvery underneath of its leaves, which turn golden yellow in autumn. Large and fast growing, its branches are often brittle and prone to breaking. Suitable for large and open spaces but never be tempted to shoehorn in restricted areas or you will inherit a maintenance nightmare.

It tolerates air pollution and wet soils. There are several examples that have reached over 30 metres in height in as little as 100 years so be sure to give it plenty of room at planting.

Mature height: 20m+

Shape of mature tree

Wet soils

# ACER saccharinum
# Laciniata Wieri

**Discovered in 1873 by DB Wier, this large spreading tree has pendulous lower branches and deeply divided sharply toothed leaves. Its large, wide limbs make it a splendid subject for parks and other open spaces.**

Like its parent plant it thrives on most soils and extreme conditions and grows with great vigour. Given enough space it can be truly dramatic but if planted for the moment rather than for the next generation you can pass on a legacy of high maintenance. Best to avoid excessively windy sites.

Mature height: 20m+

Shape of mature tree

Wet soils

# ACER saccharinum Pyramidale

**Introduced in the mid 1880s, this large, broadly pyramidal tree is best suited for parkland, open spaces and wide verges. It has heavy, ascending branches with smaller leaves than those of the species and is a good choice for verges and avenues.**

Tolerating most soils and conditions it grows about half as wide as it is tall whilst often retaining its apically dominant central leader. Like other clones of Silver Maple it is best not to manipulate by pruning as this will lead to a corrective cycle that is hard to break. Even though this could be perceived as a street form, don't be tempted as it is too vigorous and will quickly upset the pavement levels.

| 20+ Mature height: 20m+ | Shape of mature tree | Wet soils |

# AESCULUS x carnea Briotii

*Red Horse Chestnut*

This large tree is wonderful in parks and planted in avenues. Of rounded habit, it produces dark pink, almost red, flowers in May and dates back to the late 1850s. Given the Award of Garden Merit in 2002, this stately tree is a great favourite in the UK.

The fruits are smaller and less spiny, if at all, than those of the Horse Chestnut. Although they thrive in all soils and tolerate air pollution they are most impressive in early spring when the stocky strong growth bursts into life seemingly on the first warm day in April. Having said this, trees that emerge early in the spring are often on the wane by September so don't expect a glorious autumn display.

| 15|20 Mature height: 15-20m | Shape of mature tree | Avenue trees |

Telephone 01353 720 748 • www.barcham.co.uk • Fax 01353 723 060

# AESCULUS x carnea Plantierensis

Raised in France in the mid 1890s this splendid, large tree produces pale pink flowers with yellow throats in late spring. Probably the best of the carnea types it is resistant to many of the leaf afflictions that affect horse chestnuts from late summer onwards.

Raised in the famous Simon-Louis Frere nursery near Metz, it is a backcross between carnea and hippocastanum and being a triploid it does not produce fruit. It does best in large open areas and makes a stately show when planted in avenues. It thrives in all soils and tolerates air pollution but like all the species of this type it is best in the spring and early summer.

Mature height: 20m+

Shape of mature tree

Avenue trees

# AESCULUS flava

*Yellow Buckeye*

Also known as Sweet Buckeye, this medium to large tree has creamy yellow flowers marked with red – the nearest to yellow in a horse chestnut.  In its native south eastern United States it grows on river banks and mountain sides, and it was once widely used to produce paper pulp.  In Britain, it is a good choice for parks and open spaces.

It thrives in all soils, tolerates air pollution and, unusually for horse chestnut, has a good show of yellow autumn colour. Introduced from America in 1764, it won the Award of Garden Merit in 2002. The national champion in America is over 45 metres tall by 17 metres wide.

15|20
Mature height: 15-20m

Shape of mature tree

Flowering trees

# AESCULUS hippocastanum

*Horse Chestnut*

One of the most well-known and loved of all trees! Very attractive in late spring with its white, tinged yellow then pink, candle-like flowers, followed by burnished "conkers" in their spiky casings.  It originates from the borders of Greece and Albania and was introduced to Britain in the early 1600s. Wonderful in parks and open spaces.

Over recent years it has been subjected to a number of debilitating pests ranging from bleeding canker to leaf blotch and leaf miner so beware!

20+
Mature height: 20m+

Shape of mature tree

Avenue trees

# AESCULUS hippocastanum Baumannii

This cultivar was discovered by A.N. Baumann near Geneva in 1820 and was propagated as a branch sport from the mother hippocastanum tree. It is notable for its double white flowers and the fact that it does not produce "conkers", which may be seen as an advantage if required for large streets and avenues. The main branches are rather horizontal, so high pruning is required when used as a street tree.

It can commonly grow in excess of 30 metres and it is always amusing to see kids chucking objects at one in full foliage in anticipation of a shower of conkers as a reward, not knowing it is sterile. Particularly grand in the spring with its strong growth and flower display, it thrives in most soils and tolerates air pollution. Like all hippocastanum types however they are the first to wane in September prior to dormancy.

Like the rest of this genus, recent years have seen a wide range of debilitating pests and diseases that are making people think twice about planting this once much favoured tree. Leaf blotch, scale insect, leaf miner and bleeding canker may prove too much for this tremendous tree to withstand.

|  |  |  |
| --- | --- | --- |
| 20+ Mature height: 20m+ | Shape of mature tree | Avenue trees |

The further north you get in the UK the less the associated problems seem to be but our advise is to stop the avenue planting and stick to specimen individuals just in case. Baumannii's flowers herald the spring and its stout growth gives it a solid appearance.

Telephone 01353 720 748 • www.barcham.co.uk • Fax 01353 723 060

# AESCULUS indica

## *Indian Horse Chestnut*

**The Indian Horse Chestnut originates in the Himalayas, having been introduced to Britain in the 1850s and we are indebted to Henry Girling who very kindly gave us seed from the clonal selection Sydney Pearce from his garden to grow on.**

A majestic tall tree, well suited to parkland and large estates, it has a rounded habit. It bears pyramidal panicles of pink flushed flowers in summer, while its foliage is bronze when young, turning glossy and dark green before changing to orange and yellow in autumn. It tolerates chalky soils well.

There has been increased incidence of what was thought to be Phytophthora bleeding canker on Horse Chestnuts, especially in the South East and Midlands of England. Research is ongoing but it is now believed the cause is a bacterium rather than a fungus, but feedback from arborists suggests Aesculus indica has immunity from the infection. However, it is not a common tree so the jury is out on this one.

Mature height: 20m

Shape of mature tree

Avenue trees

Its deeply cut leaves make it the prettiest of the Chestnut family but annoyingly it sometimes sets flower on the terminal growing bud, making it difficult to grow straight. However this is our problem to resolve, not yours!

# AILANTHUS altissima

## *Tree of Heaven*

Introduced in 1751, this fast growing native of Northern China was said to reach for the sky. In hot summers it is quick to naturalise and it can make fun of growing in truly inhospitable urban or rural environments.

Living up to its common name, it is certainly large and broadly columnar in habit. Although not botanically related, it produces long, ash-like foliage. Tolerant of air pollution and ideal for street plantings where space permits, it is best suited on wide verges or central reservations. It thrives in most soils.

| Mature height: 20m+ | Shape of mature tree | Urban trees |

# ALBIZIA julibrissin Umbrella

## *Silk Tree*

**A native of Iran and China, this small and compact form tolerates our climate only if planted in protected and south facing southern England.**

The foliage is very exotic, resembling that of mimosa, and the profuse pink fluffy flowers are particularly effective in hot dry summers. Unlike many of our native trees, this introduction thrives with reflective heat bouncing off buildings and pavements so is very usefully planted as a street tree in London where it is sheltered but subjected to stifling heat .

| Mature height: 5-10m | Shape of mature tree | Flowering trees |

● Telephone 01353 720 748 ● www.barcham.co.uk ● Fax 01353 723 060

# ALNUS cordata

## *Italian Alder*

Originating in southern Italy and introduced in 1820, this fast growing, medium tree has a conical habit. Its shiny, green, pear-like leaves last well into winter, particularly under street lighting. It produces notably larger fruits than other alders. Good for parks and verges, we also recommend it for coastal plantings.

It thrives on all ground including dry, high ph soils but is most at home nearest water. Being highly tolerant of urban pollution it is a particularly adaptable urban tree but must be given enough room or it can outstay its welcome. Italian trials indicate that it can even tolerate acid rain. The bark is a glistening brown when young but matures to be rougher.

Once heralded by many as the perfect candidate for an urban tree, its vigour can cause the lifting of hard areas over time so I would advise planting on verges rather than paved streets where it can outplay its welcome.

Mature height: 15-20m

Shape of mature tree

Clay soils

# ALNUS glutinosa
## *Common Alder*

**Once used for the production of clogs in northern England, this medium sized native tree has a conical growth habit and produces yellow catkins in March. Its natural habitat is boggy land and river banks. However it is also very good for urban plantings as it thrives in all soils and tolerates air pollution. Available as both multi-stemmed and as a single stem.**

Being a native tree, it is a wonderful host to a wide range of wildlife. It is a very useful variety to plant where the ground is liable to flood and survives many weeks with its roots underwater. There was a scare about Alder being susceptible to Phytophthora along water courses up and down the country but this was highly overstated and Alnus glutinosa remains a vital inclusion to any native planting mix.

In its early years Common Alder can grow very quickly, sometimes putting on over two metres of growth in a single growing season when the availability of water coupled with high temperatures predominate. A great tree for use as a screen, it is often seen flanking orchards for this reason.

| 15|20 | | | |
|---|---|---|---|
| Mature height: 15-20m | Shape of mature tree | Multi-stem | Wet soils |

● Telephone 01353 720 748   ● www.barcham.co.uk   ● Fax 01353 723 060

# ALNUS glutinosa
## Imperialis / Laciniata

Introduced in the 1860s, this cultivar has finely cut leaves and won the Award of Merit in 1973. A tree of medium size, it has a graceful, conical habit, and is very good for broad verges and for parks. We have also seen it used both in Leicester and Liverpool as a very effective street tree.

**Strictly speaking Imperialis and Laciniata are two different, though very similar, clones. However they have been inextricably mixed in the trade over the years making it unclear which is which so we list them together. Certainly the difference between them is not worth worrying about! It thrives in all soils and tolerates air pollution. Being a variation of a native tree, the cut leaves make this truly striking.**

Mature height: 15-20m

Shape of mature tree

Wet soils

# ALNUS incana

*Grey Alder*

A really hardy and tough medium tree, capable of coping with cold, wet soils and exposed situations. Grey alder is a fast grower, well suited to industrial areas and street plantings. Its pointed grey leaves readily distinguish it from Alnus glutinosa.

Introduced from Europe in the 1780s it does best on calcareous soils and tolerates air pollution. In the recent past the North American tree bearing the same generic name has been changed to Alnus rugosa to avoid confusion amongst well travelled tree enthusiasts. Profuse pink / yellow catkins are produced just prior to spring.

Mature height: 15-20m

Shape of mature tree

Wet soils

# ALNUS incana Aurea

**Winning the Award of Merit in 1995 and introduced in the early 1860s, this magnificent small tree is a must for any garden in need of winter interest. Unlike the species, this is a slow grower. It does best in moist soil and semi-shaded areas.**

The young shoots and leaves emerge a golden yellow in spring which contrast beautifully with vivid red catkins that open to a pink / yellow. The catkins form as early as August and get better and better in colour and size throughout the winter. The bark and twiggy branches also turn orange during the winter. Good as a street tree and for parks and gardens.

As the catkins show so early this is one of the few trees we have that can legitimately offer all year round interest. It has always been underplayed by growers but we have been bulking up our numbers over recent years to market it effectively. Quick to grow when juvenile, it is far more sedate in growth at maturity that its parent, Alnus incana, so is an ideal subject for a garden.

| 5\|10 | | |
| --- | --- | --- |
| Mature height: 5-10m | Shape of mature tree | Yellow foliage |

This lovely clone can provide wonderful contrast within a garden so care should be taken on where to site it. On frosty or even snowy winter days its vivid red catkin display can be simply stunning. Similarly its light coloured foliage can brighten a dour evergreen backdrop.

● Telephone 01353 720 748  ● www.barcham.co.uk  ● Fax 01353 723 060

# ALNUS incana
# Laciniata

Introduced in the early 1860s this superb cut leaf form won the First Class Certificate in 1873. A medium tree with dissected leaves, it has a conical habit when mature and is most attractive. Equally at home in a street, park, verge or garden.

It does best in moist soil but can tolerate the vagaries of urban conditions. There is not much to choose between this variety and the cut leaf forms of Alnus glutinosa as all are remarkably striking and probably the pick of all the cut leaved trees we offer.

| 10\|15 | | |
|---|---|---|
| Mature height: 10-15m | Shape of mature tree | Wet soils |

I have seen this tree used most effectively in several towns and cities in the UK. The selections in Liverpool have outstripped expectation and must be between 12 and 15 metres tall. Their pyramidal crowns are lovely in season as the cut leaves give it a very soft and graceful appearance. Best specimens are usually found in the west as annual rainfall is higher.

● Telephone 01353 720 748   ● www.barcham.co.uk   ● Fax 01353 723 060

# ALNUS spaethii

Of garden origin and dating from 1908, this fast growing tree of medium size has a rounded habit and is good as a park and street tree. It will also tolerate coastal conditions. The large leaves are purple tinged when young and it is at its best in spring when displaying its beautiful and numerous catkins.

It does best in moist soil, though can cope with dry soils once established, and tolerates air pollution. This variety catches many of our customers out in that it looks like a cherry when in full leaf in the summer. The leaves are vivid green and large as well as being long. The bark gives the game away but this is always a good tree to throw into a plant identification competition for the over confident!

A cross between Alnus japonica and Alnus subcordata, it is little surprise that this is a rarely seen tree but in our opinion it could and should be used more often to bring greater diversity to Alnus plantings in the UK. Its catkin display is second to none amongst the large growing Alders more regularly planted.

| 15|20 | | |
|---|---|---|
| Mature height: 15-20m | Shape of mature tree | Wet soils |

# AMELANCHIER arborea
# Robin Hill

*Serviceberry*

A wonderful small tree that we consider to be by far the best tree form of Serviceberry on the market. It forms a dense, oval habit and produces its masses of spring flowers that open pink and turn white. A North American selection and as highly rated there as it is here. I have planted one outside of my office window at Barcham so I am rarely far away from this tree!

The young leaves emerge coppery red and then harden to green by late spring before they turn vivid red in autumn.

A very good choice for street plantings and residential areas as it provides plenty of interest with virtually no maintenance. Being such a small tree of ultimate size, it can be placed much closer to buildings than most trees which make it a fantastic choice for urban planting. There are very few trees that offer wonderful floral displays in the spring and glorious autumn leaf colour but this is one of them. It does best in moist, well drained, lime free soils.

| 5|10 | | |
|---|---|---|
| Mature height: 5-10m | Shape of mature tree | Flowering trees |

We latched onto this clone in the late 1990s and there are now some fine examples of how they progress at maturity. It makes a fantastic small urban tree suitable for both streets and gardens and its seasonal interest makes it one of the glamour trees of our range.

# AMELANCHIER
# Ballerina

*Serviceberry*

**This small tree, with its finely toothed leaves, was selected by the Experimental Station at Boskoop in the Netherlands in the 1970s and named in 1980. It forms a broader crown than Robin Hill and is less tall making it a better choice for verges and gardens than it is for streets.**

It has abundant white flowers in spring and excellent red autumn colour. It does best in moist, well drained, lime free soils and is remarkably resistant to fire blight. It won the Award of Garden Merit in 2002 and remains a great choice for any garden. Sometimes grown as a bushy shrub, we train ours to tree form with a 1.5-1.8m clear stem with a well defined central stem and rounded crown.

A hybrid of Amelanchier laevis, its flowers are larger than 'Robin Hill' or lamarckii making it a very showy performer in the spring. Its fruits are edible and are a particular favourite of blackbirds in my garden. Its spreading crown gives it a more rustic feel than 'Robin Hill' making it more suited to rural gardens.

5|10
Mature height:
5-10m

Shape of
mature tree

Flowering
trees

● Telephone 01353 720 748  ● www.barcham.co.uk  ● Fax 01353 723 060

# AMELANCHIER
## lamarckii

*Serviceberry*

Naturalised over much of Western Europe, it is a simply stunning sight when in full bloom with its white flowers produced in plentiful racemes. It is a small, shrubby tree with emerging copper coloured leaves turning green by late spring before they mature to a rich red as autumn progresses. The rounded fruits, red in summer before turning black in autumn, are edible.

Although we grow this both as a multi stem and single stemmed tree please be aware that if you buy the latter form it is prone to sucker and broaden with age so requiring far more maintenance than Robin Hill if planted as a street tree. In our opinion it makes a far better subject if planted as a coppiced multi-stem tree for verge or garden plantings as you maximise its flowering potential and are going with its natural habit. It does best in moist, well drained, lime free soils. Fine near buildings, I have one growing happily two metres from my front door!

| 5\|7 | | | |
|---|---|---|---|
| Mature height: 5-7m | Shape of mature tree | Multi-stem | Flowering trees |

# ARALIA elata
## *Japanese Angelica Tree*

Introduced to Britain in the 1830s from its native Japan, it won the Award of Merit in 1959 and the Award of Garden Merit in 2002. A remarkably odd looking tree, wonderfully exotic in foliage which falls away in autumn to leave only a few spiky branches.

It makes a small rounded tree and is remarkable for its very large, doubly pinnate leaves, produced mainly in a "ruff" towards the tips of its stems. The foliage often gives vivid and luminous autumn colour, coinciding with its extraordinary stunning display of white panicle flowers.

Mature height: 5-10m

Shape of mature tree

Flowering trees

# ARAUCARIA araucana
## *Monkey Puzzle*

Sometimes referred to as the Chile Pine it is also a native of Argentina. This ancient slow growing evergreen tree is well known for its distinctive long slender branches that are densely covered with overlapping spiked leaves. Introduced into the UK in 1795 by Archibald Menzies, the famous Navy surgeon who later turned plant collector, it won the Award of Merit in 1980. Amazingly enough, it was once a native of Britain. The fossilized wood from this tree was highly coveted by Queen Victoria. Otherwise known as Jet, it was used in the making of mourning jewellery.

**Hardy in the UK, they are often planted far too close to houses so have to be removed before they get to maturity. This unusual conifer prefers a moist loamy soil and has great apical dominance drawing the tree up strongly vertical so it is very suited to crown lifting. Try not to handle the foliage unless you are well protected as the leaves are very sharp! The cones are globular, up to 20cm in length and take up to three years to mature.**

Mature height: 20m+

Shape of mature tree

Evergreen trees

● Telephone 01353 720 748 ● www.barcham.co.uk ● Fax 01353 723 060

# ARBUTUS unedo

## *Killarney Strawberry Tree*

**This native of South West Ireland and the Mediterranean is, unusually for an ericaceous plant, tolerant of lime. It is a small evergreen with brown, shedding bark, and its flowers and fruits are produced together in the autumn. A good choice for exposed and coastal sites, it is also good for urban plantings.**

A winner of the Award of Garden Merit in 2002 and of a First Class Certificate in 1933, it does well in most soil types, but prefers it moist. Don't be afraid to hard prune if getting untidy, as if this is done in late March / April it grows back beautifully. We grow it as both a bushy shrub and a full standard tree. Young shoots are tinged red which contrasts well against the dark green leaves.

Mature height:
5-10m

Shape of
mature tree

Evergreen
trees

# BETULA albosinensis Fascination
## *Chinese Birch*

The species from which Fascination was developed was brought back from China in 1901 by Ernest Wilson. He was very taken with it, describing it as follows:

**"The bark is singularly lovely, being a rich orange-red or orange-brown and peels off in sheets, each no thicker than fine tissue paper, and each successive layer is clothed with a white glaucous bloom"**

Further to this the catkins in the spring are amazing, up to 10cm in length, opening to a rich yellow-brown and so numerous my kids call it the 'caterpillar tree'.

10|15
Mature height: 10-15m

Shape of mature tree

Bark interest

Fascination is a refined clone with dark green leaves, which are large for a birch, appearing in April, along with the showy display of yellow catkins. It has outstanding stem colour – orange peeling to pink and cream and then purest white once the tree gets beyond 30cm girth. It is a medium sized tree, becoming oval as it matures, has stiffly ascending branches and the one outside my kitchen window, now over 50cm girth, is a constant joy and often commented on. A great choice for parks and verges growing well on most soils. It is listed by a few as Betula utilis Fascination but we put it firmly classified in the albosinensis group.

Telephone 01353 720 748 • www.barcham.co.uk • Fax 01353 723 060

# BETULA ermanii (Holland)
## *Erman Birch*

This birch was originally from North East Asia and Japan and was first cultivated in the 1880s. Always the first tree to emerge with new leaf in the spring at Barcham, and one of the first to fall in autumn. Importantly it tolerates reflected heat and light very adequately so is a great urban tree that requires little maintenance.

An elegant and vigorous medium to large tree, the bright green, often heart shaped and prominently veined leaves which appear very early in spring become clear yellow in autumn. It grows well on most soils.

| 15\|20 | | |
|---|---|---|
| Mature height: 15-20m | Shape of mature tree | Bark interest |

# BETULA nigra (Heritage)
## *River Birch*

Also known as the Red Birch, this is one of the very best trees for wet soils and we favour the clonal selection from the States called Heritage, selected in 1968, for its vigour and uniformity. Originally found along the river banks of the South Eastern United States, this medium sized tree makes a great show with its shaggy, flaking, cinnamon / orange bark. Mature trees are truly statuesque and broadly pyramidal in form. Foliage is soft green and diamond shaped.

Its common name of River Birch is misleading as we have seen this tree thriving in arid London tree pits. Once established, it can tolerate extreme heat in the summer, thriving in Florida as well as Kentucky in the States. This could become a good choice for the South East of the UK as temperatures continue to break records during the summer months. Available as both a standard tree and as a multi-stem.

| 15\|20 | | |
|---|---|---|
| Mature height: 15-20m | Shape of mature tree | Bark interest |

# BETULA maximowicziana
*Monarch Birch*

An oddity within our Birch range, hardly looking like a member of the same family. It is a native of Japan where it can reach up to 35 metres in height but it is rare to see in the UK and reaches a more modest height of between 15-20cm. Introduced into the UK in 1893, this is one to catch someone out on a tree identification competition.

**It is fast growing and has a dark brown trunk when young, maturing into greyish tinges. The large heart shaped leaves turn clear yellow in the autumn. It retains a pyramidal shape when young but this broadens at maturity. The leaves are the biggest of all the Birch family, sometimes attaining over 12cm in length.**

Mature height: 15-20m    Shape of mature tree    Avenue trees

# BETULA papyrifera
*Paper Birch*

The Paper Birch is also known as the Canoe Birch in its native North America and was introduced into the UK in 1750. Until it clears 20-25cm girth the bark is a brown / red and very distinguishable from other juvenile birch but after this point the bark starts to whiten markedly. A pioneer species, particularly quick to colonise areas devastated by fire.

The waterproof qualities of its bark made it an important tree for the Native Americans who used it for making canoes and wigwam covers, as well as eating utensils. It makes a medium to large tree with a conical habit. It has white, papery bark, the colour being carried high into the canopy, and attractive yellow autumn foliage. One of the most elegant of trees for parks. It does best on moist, well drained sandy soil, but is tolerant of most conditions.

Mature height: 15-20m    Shape of mature tree    Bark interest

Telephone 01353 720 748   www.barcham.co.uk   Fax 01353 723 060

Barcham

# BETULA pendula
*Silver Birch*

The Silver Birch is also known as the "Lady of the Woods" – so called because of its slender and graceful appearance. It is a pioneer species and particularly admired in the UK. Even though it seemingly grows anywhere it is remarkably difficult to successfully transplant bare rooted but our containerised trees solve this problem. A group of three silver birches that we supplied were planted in Stamford, Lincolnshire in 2005 and have grown from 12-14cm girth to 20-25cm girth in three years!

## *Silver Birch*

A medium tree with a conical, but semi weeping habit, the bark is white with horizontal lines and large, diamond shaped cracks as the tree matures. Very good for parks and woodland, but not suitable for areas where soil becomes compacted. It grows well on most soils and we grow it as both a single stemmed tree and a multi-stemmed tree.

Multi-stemmed trees are particularly useful when planted on elevated or exposed ground as they have a low centre of gravity and need no staking. Our multi-stemmed birch is grown as true single plant coppices, not three or four plants bundled together in a pot that can lead to issues further down the line.

**15|20**
Mature height: 15-20m

Shape of mature tree

Multi-stem

Native trees

# BETULA pendula Dalecarlica
*Swedish Birch*

A most elegant tree and perfect for specimen planting. For those of you that went to Writtle Agricultural College you will remember the splendid short avenue of them leading to the refectory block. Some call this clone 'Laciniata' or 'Crispa' but don't worry about it as the differences are too slight to cause a dilemma.

Found in Sweden in the 1760s, it is a medium to large tree of slender form and with a broadly columnar habit. The leaves are deeply cut and branches weep gracefully. Bark is white and peeling. Very good for parks and woodland, but not suitable for areas where soil becomes compacted or where there is too much reflected heat and light. It grows well on most soils.

It is always good to bear in mind a tree's origin to assess its physiology. Sweden has shorter day lengths than southern England so to place this clone in a paved area in London would represent extreme conditions for this tree. It is much happier planted in greener areas and further north.

| 15\|20 | Shape of mature tree | Bark interest |
| --- | --- | --- |
| Mature height: 10-15m | | |

# BETULA pendula Fastigiata

An upright form of the Silver Birch, resembling the shape of a Lombardy Poplar. It tends to spiral its way upwards giving a corkscrew effect of twiggy birch branches that hold their leaves slightly longer than most other varieties. The bark, although similar to Betula pendula is not as spectacular as the white barked clones.

This medium to large tree has stiffly ascending branches which give it a columnar habit. In cultivation since the 1870s, it makes a good street and car park tree as it requires little space. It grows well on most soils and the highest recorded specimen comes in at over 30 metres although I have never seen any at half that size.

| 10\|15 | Shape of mature tree | Narrow trees |
| --- | --- | --- |
| Mature height: 10-15m | | |

● Telephone 01353 720 748  ● www.barcham.co.uk  ● Fax 01353 723 060

# BETULA pendula Purpurea
## *Purple Birch*

**Introduced in the early 1870s, this slow growing and rare variety won the First Class Certificate in 1874. One of the largest specimens I have seen happens to be in my next door neighbour's garden in Rutland and has reached over 10 metres whilst retaining a slender habit.**

Dark purple leaves emerge in spring soften to a dark green / purple by summer. The bark is similar to that of Betula pendula and the habit is similarly repeated. It will grow on most soils and is best suited for gardens and arboretums.

| 15\|20 | | |
|---|---|---|
| Mature height: 15-20m | Shape of mature tree | Red/purple foliage |

# BETULA pendula Tristis
## *Weeping Birch*

Introduced in 1867 this outstanding cultivar won the Award of Garden Merit in 2002. It is a sight to behold in winter when its twiggy growth, supported on pendulous limbs, are shrouded in frost on a bright morning. If space is restricted, or for small gardens, Betula pendula Youngii should be chosen instead.

A most graceful and particularly beautiful tall tree, with slender, pendent branches. Although a weeping birch, it maintains a central leader, and is excellent planted as a specimen. Also good for wide verges and avenues, it grows well on most soils. The bark matures to a decent white making this, in our opinion, one of the best tall weeping trees on the market.

I think this tree is at its best when it stands still and dormant in winter with a severe frost covering its fine cascading twiggy branches.

| 20 | | |
|---|---|---|
| Mature height: 20m | Shape of mature tree | Bark interest |

# BETULA pendula Youngii
*Young's Weeping Birch*

Originating in the early 1870s, this small to medium weeping birch has no defined central leader and therefore eventually forms an attractive dome shape. Sometimes produced top worked to get the initial height, we prefer to grow a structurally stronger plant from the base and draw up a leader until we have formed a 1.8-2 metre clear stem that can support the crown thereafter.

The thin branches eventually reach the ground and the serrated, triangular leaves show good autumn colour. It develops a smooth white bark and is an attractive specimen tree for lawns. It grows well on most soils and has been a great favourite in the UK for many years.

Mature height: 5-7m

Shape of mature tree

Bark interest

● Telephone 01353 720 748  ● www.barcham.co.uk  ● Fax 01353 723 060

# BETULA pubescens
## *Common White Birch*

The Common White Birch is also known as Downy Birch and Hairy Birch. Oil from its stem is used in the production of leather, while the bark was once used for roofing in Scandinavia. A native of both the UK and Europe, it ideally prefers damper soils than Betula pendula so is more commonly seen in the west. In our opinion it is an undervalued tree for planting in the general landscape and should be used more frequently ahead of the more popular Silver Birch.

Linnaeus classed this with Betula pendula, but it differs in not having pendulous branches and in having darker bark and downy young shoots. The white bark peels into papery layers, but does not have the characteristic diamond shaped cracks of Silver Birch. Very good for parks and verges. It grows well on most soils.

Mature height:
15-20m

Shape of
mature tree

Bark
interest

To vouch for its hardiness, Betula pubescens can be seen growing further north than any other broadleaf tree. It generally forms a scrubby low lying tree at this latitude and is native of both Greenland and Iceland. Its ascending branches give it a more solid appearance than Betula pendula and this makes it a tougher prospect to grow on exposed sites.

# BETULA utilis Jacquemontii / Doorenbos

There are now so many differing clones put under this banner that the trade is tying itself in knots of confusion, but suffice it to say if you are after the gleaming white barked birch under the above cultivar name from Barcham you will not be disappointed! The unsurpassed whiteness of the trunk and branches peels routinely each year and is accentuated by lenticel lines.

A native of the western Himalayas, it makes a medium tree with ascending branches, and is also spectacular when grown as a multi-stem. However, beware those growers who palm off a multi-stem as three separate trees grown together as this will only lead to structural problems later on. Its oval, dark green leaves turn golden yellow in autumn.

Excellent for urban plantings, it grows well on most soils.

Mature height: 15-20m

Shape of mature tree

Multi-stem

Bark interest

Some nurseries have tried growing this clone through micro propagation but the results at maturity are more than disappointing, with a loose and poor crown formation. We strongly recommend a budded / grafted plant as the result is proven and the mature crown structure assured.

Telephone 01353 720 748 • www.barcham.co.uk • Fax 01353 723 060

# BETULA utilis Long Trunk

This botanical oddity is a tricky one to describe as it possesses so many traits of unrelated cultivars. I suppose a habit of Betula pendula Youngii with the same measure of Betula pendula Tristis on a tree with Betula utilis Jacquemontii trunk and leaves sums it up. The combination makes it an ideal candidate for gardens or parks.

This small to medium sized tree has glistening white bark, which routinely peels each year to make it look even more attractive. Its oval, dark green leaves turn golden yellow in autumn. It has a weeping habit but possesses enough apical dominance to keep growing upwards so retaining a relatively slender and not mushroomed habit. It is tolerant of most soils.

| 5\|10 | | |
|---|---|---|
| Mature height: 5-10m | Shape of mature tree | Bark interest |

# BROUSSONETIA papyrifera
*Paper Mulberry*

Introduced in the early 18th century and now naturalised in America, fibre from the Paper Mulberry was once woven into a fine cloth in Polynesia and its bark is still processed to make paper in its native Japan. In Europe it is regarded as a highly ornamental specimen tree suitable for gardens, parks and arboretums.

| 10\|15 | | |
|---|---|---|
| Mature height: 10-15m | Shape of mature tree | Bark interest |

A small to medium tree, it has lobed, hairy leaves, no two of which are the same shape. Male plants have pendent catkins, while the females bear orange-red fruits. The young stems are green and brown blotched giving it a somewhat unusual camouflaged effect. Tied to the same family as Morus, this is one for the plant collector. It does best on fertile, calcareous soil.

● Telephone 01353 720 748 ● www.barcham.co.uk ● Fax 01353 723 060

Barcham

# BUTTA capitata
## *Jelly Palm*

A native of Brazil and Uruguay, this small palm slowly makes a tree about 5 metres tall. Best suited for protected south facing aspects of southern England where it counts as a very exotic addition to any plant collection.

The stout trunk is shrouded by the remains of old leaves as the palm matures and the very large succulent leaves are a bluish grey, sometimes as long as 75cm. Mature plants produce numerous small yellow to red flowers that are followed by oval yellow / orange fruits about 2-3cm in length.

Mature height: 5-7m

Shape of mature tree

Garden trees

# BUXUS sempervirens Arborescens
## *Box*

**This large shrub can occasionally be classified as a small tree and is a clonal selection of common box that won the Award of Garden Merit in 2002.**

The small but numerous evergreen leaves make this plant an ideal subject for screening / hedging. If left unclipped it will eventually reach approximately 7 metres after about 40 years. For those of you that enjoy topiary, this is an ideal candidate. It thrives on most soils and doesn't mind both sun and shade.

Mature height: 5-7m

Shape of mature tree

Garden trees

# CALLISTEMON laevis
*Bottle Brush*

This beautiful small tree is a native of Australia and Tasmania but is only suitable for sites where it rarely dips below -2 Celsius. Sheltered London piazzas and sun trapped urban gardens are prime locations to enjoy the superb flowering display this small tree offers.

Although mostly available as a shrub, we grow this as a full standard tree. The intense red flowers are produced by mid summer and are abundant as well as absolutely stunning. The evergreen crown of fine green leaves benefits from a tidying prune every spring to keep the crown compact and to stimulate vigour and flower. Suited to most soils, though best to avoid shallow chalk.

They are often hard to overwinter outside when small, but by the time they reach a girthing size they are better equipped to take an English winter. Be sure to buy from nurseries that have overwintered them outside rather than in a glasshouse to get a tree well adjusted to take the cold. Similarly, beware stock imported from Italy as it could be set back hard before it has the chance to acclimatize.

Mature height: 5m | Shape of mature tree | Flowering trees

# CALOCEDRUS decurrens
*Incense Cedar*

Native to California and Oregon, this large, evergreen conifer has a columnar habit making it unmistakable. Introduced in 1853, it won the Award of Garden Merit in 2002. Resembling Thuja when young, this superb truly fastigiate conifer is often overlooked but it makes a fabulous impact in garden, verge or park with no ongoing maintenance issues.

**Perfect as a specimen tree or grown in avenues, it has dark green leaves crowded into fan-like sprays with oval, hanging cones. It grows well on most soils and is well suited to growing in the UK.**

Mature height: 15-20m | Shape of mature tree | Evergreen trees

● Telephone 01353 720 748 ● www.barcham.co.uk ● Fax 01353 723 060

# CAMELLIA sasanqua Rosea

**Introduced in the early 1800s and a native of China and Japan, this acid loving small evergreen tree is grown at Barcham as a full standard.**

It is better planted in the south facing gardens of southern England where it thrives to make a small tree about 5 metres in height. Glossy evergreen leaves are beautifully contrasted with luscious pink fragrant flowers in both autumn and spring. Generally, the hotter the preceding summer, the better the performance. It is also best to position the plant in a sheltered spot, protecting it against cold winter winds.

Mature height:
5-7m

Shape of
mature tree

Flowering
trees

# CARPINUS betulus

*Hornbeam*

The timber of the Hornbeam has traditionally been used to produce mallets, skittles and even the moving parts of pianos. Winning the Award of Garden Merit in 2002, this wonderful native tree is closely related to the hop hornbeam, Ostrya carpinifolia.

Wonderful in a parkland setting, growing in groups and ideal for pleaching, the Hornbeam is a large tree with a characteristic grey fluted trunk and ovate, ribbed and serrated leaves which turn a lovely clear yellow in autumn. This British native produces hard, finely grained timber with many uses. It grows well on most soils, including clay and chalk. A most useful tree for poor planting conditions.

15|20
Mature height:
15-20m

Shape of
mature tree

Native
trees

# CARPINUS betulus Fastigiata

This Hornbeam received an Award of Garden Merit from the Royal Horticultural Society in 2002. A tree of medium size and pyramidal habit. Slender in its youth, it can often be seen growing in restricted areas despite the fact that it develops "middle age spread", reaching up to 10m wide. It is better growing in an open, parkland setting and is very effective if left feathered to the base, producing gold and orange autumn colours. It grows well on most soils, including clay and chalk. A most useful tree for poor planting conditions.

**In our opinion this clone should be renamed Carpinus betulus Globosum and if care isn't taken when selecting, some are very difficult to prune and manage when older. Always look out for a straight central trunk tapering to a well defined leader because if the main stem is supplied co-dominant at a low level the tree can never be satisfactorily crown lifted at maturity and the tree gently becomes wider and wider.**

10|15

Mature height:
10-15m

Shape of
mature tree

Clay
soils

For those impatient amongst you, the denser ascending branches can be used to form an instant hedge. Simply plant a four year old tree at two metre centres and hedge trim the tops to achieve immediate privacy.

● Telephone 01353 720 748  ● www.barcham.co.uk  ● Fax 01353 723 060

# CARPINUS betulus Fastigiata Frans Fontaine

This Hornbeam cultivar was selected from a street in the Netherlands in the early 1980s. A far better proposition for planting in restricted areas than Carpinus betulus Fastigiata, it retains its columnar habit, being only 3m wide after 25 years. It tolerates pollution and soil compaction, so makes an excellent street tree. It grows well on most soils, including clay and chalk. A most useful tree for poor planting conditions.

Frans Fontaine is very similar to Carpinus betulus Fastigiata when small and we often get called to describe the differences. The former sometimes has a rough fissured bark at the base of the main stem and its leaves are more crinkly than the latter.

**10|15**
Mature height:
10-15m

Shape of
mature tree

Urban
trees

# CARPINUS japonica
*Japanese Hornbeam*

Introduced from Japan in 1895, this small tree won the Award of Garden Merit in 2002. It is particularly effective when used for pleaching as the spreading horizontal branches can be easily trained and the flowering hop display along their length is a fantastic bonus compared to using native hornbeam for the same purpose.

A most beautiful and widely spreading, rounded small tree, it has heavily corrugated foliage, which is darker than the European Hornbeam, and attractive fruiting catkins which resemble hops. An excellent park tree, it has smooth, pink / grey bark. It grows well on most soils, including clay and chalk. A most useful and pretty tree for poor planting conditions.

**5|10**
Mature height:
5-10m

Shape of
mature tree

Garden
trees

# CASTANEA sativa

*Sweet Chestnut*

Chestnuts roasting on an open fire – or bought piping hot from a street vendor – so evocative of Christmas long ago! Believed to have been introduced by the Romans, this tree is native of Southern Europe and North Africa but has long been naturalised in the UK. It won the Award of Garden Merit in 2002. Its spiralling rough bark at maturity is lovely.

A versatile and beautiful, fast growing, large tree, which is particularly attractive in early summer when laden with its male and female catkins. Its long, glossy leaves turn gold and bronze before falling. The timber is highly prized around the Mediterranean and in Provence much furniture is made from chestnut wood. A splendid tree for grouping and quite outstanding planted as an avenue. It does best on reasonably dry, light soils, and is moderately lime tolerant.

There are many glorious specimens of this tree in the UK including within the fabulous parkland landscape at Burghley House, near Stamford, in Lincolnshire.

Mature height: 20m+ | Shape of mature tree | Avenue trees

# CASTANEA sativa Variegata

A beautiful sweet chestnut that grows slower and is of a smaller ultimate size that its parent. There used to be some wonderful examples of this cultivar at Petworth House in West Sussex that had over 4 metre trunk diameters but sadly they were ruined by the hurricane of 1987. A winner of the Award of Garden Merit in both 1964 and 2002.

Similar in most respects to the species, but with yellow edged leaves. Its distinctive foliage makes it very good as a specimen tree. Sweet chestnuts can be very long lived and are drought resistant, so are a good choice for light soils. It does best on reasonably dry, light soils, and is moderately lime tolerant.

Mature height: 15-20m | Shape of mature tree | Variegated trees

Telephone 01353 720 748 • www.barcham.co.uk • Fax 01353 723 060

# CATALPA bignonioides
*Indian Bean Tree*

From the south eastern United States comes this magnificent, medium to large tree, which is very good as an urban subject, but not in paved areas. Introduced in 1726, this eye catching tree won the Award of Garden Merit in 2002 and there are fine specimens in Palace Yard, Westminster.

|  |  |  |
|---|---|---|
| 15\|20 Mature height: 15-20m | Shape of mature tree | Flowering trees |

## Indian Bean Tree

It is late into leaf and produces exotic, orchid-like flowers in midsummer. These are followed by the "beans", which look like dark vanilla pods, in autumn. Outstanding as a specimen tree and tolerant of air pollution. It does well on most soils but avoid windy exposed sites as the large fleshy leaves can bruise.

# CATALPA bignonioides Aurea

**This golden leaved form of the superb Indian Bean Tree was introduced in the late 1870s and won the Award of Merit in 1974. Like most yellow leaved trees, it is best placed in a south facing aspect as shade tends to dull the leaf colour to a light green.**

Its large fleshy golden yellow leaves turn to a yellow green by the time the flowers open in summer. Often top worked it forms a broadly rounded crown at maturity. It is suitable for urban plantings, does best in a sheltered position and does well on most soils.

|  |  |  |
|---|---|---|
| 15\|20 Mature height: 15-20m | Shape of mature tree | Yellow foliage |

## Atlas Cedar

Very difficult to transplant as bare-rooted or root-balled, our Light Pots solve this problem and facilitate good establishment.

# CEDRUS atlantica
*Atlas Cedar*

**Introduced in the 1840s, Atlas Cedars make most imposing and stately subjects – perfect for large estates. To the untrained eye it is too similar to Cedrus libani to call and the Dutch try and clear the trade of confusion by listing it as Cedrus libani Atlantica as a catchall. We list it separately for the sake of purity!**

This large, evergreen tree from the Atlas Mountains of Algeria and Morocco forms an impressive structure of wide, horizontal branches when mature. It grows rapidly in its early years and is regarded by many as a classical parkland tree. It thrives on most soils but is better equipped to withstand urban pollution compared to Cedrus libani or deodara. Cones, 5-7 cm in length, are produced along its numerous branches.

Mature height: 20m+

Shape of mature tree

Evergreen trees

We always think of this superb tree as an individual specimen but in their native habitat they can form imposing forests on mountainsides at an altitude of 1000 metres to 2200 metres. These forests still sustain the endangered Barbary Macaque.

● Telephone 01353 720 748  ● www.barcham.co.uk  ● Fax 01353 723 060

# CEDRUS atlantica Glauca
*Blue Cedar*

The Blue Cedar is probably the most dramatic and striking of all blue conifers. A winner of both the First Class Certificate in 1972 and the Award of Garden Merit in 2002, it is both quick growing and sparsely furnished when young but thickens out with time.

This is another superb subject for specimen and parkland planting, where its form can be best appreciated. Its silvery blue foliage is very attractive but if it suffers stress during the establishment phase after planting, it can lose its leaves. This is alarming for an evergreen plant but it is fairly tough and usually reflushes the following spring. It thrives on most soils but doesn't appreciate waterlogged ground.

Mature height: 20m+ | Shape of mature tree | Evergreen trees

# CEDRUS deodara
*Deodar Cedar*

The Deodar Cedar is grown for its timber in parts of southern Europe, but is grown as an ornamental in Britain. Its root system is more fibrous and compact than that of Cedrus atlantica and libani so is often used as the rootstock for these species to avoid transplantation issues. This was pioneered by Belgium growers but they didn't account for the fact that deodara is not as long lived so we favour plants grown from seedlings. Brought from the Himalayas in the reign of George IV in 1831, this soon became a favourite planted on the lawns of large country houses and Georgian rectories. Different from all other cedars due to its trailing leader, this large, evergreen conifer has a gently pendulous habit and soft, blue / green foliage. It thrives on most soils but does not do as well in wet ground with poor drainage.

Mature height: 20m+ | Shape of mature tree | Evergreen trees

# CEDRUS deodara Karl Fuchs

This form of the Deodar Cedar is named after the German plant collector who brought the seed back from the Paktia province of Afghanistan in the 1970s. Several blue needled clones have been introduced for their increased hardiness and this is the pick of them although its toughness is not needed for the temperate UK.

Extremely hardy, and remarkable for its splendid blue foliage. Different from all other Cedars due to its trailing leader, this large, evergreen conifer has a gently pendulous habit, and is a great choice for parkland settings and large estates. It thrives on most soils but like most evergreens does not thrive in wet ground.

| 20+ | | |
|---|---|---|
| Mature height: 20m+ | Shape of mature tree | Evergreen trees |

# CEDRUS deodara Kelly Gold

This Deodar Cedar is most impressive for large gardens, parkland and estates. Like many yellow flushing varieties, this lovely conifer can be used as a focal point in the landscape in the spring with its bright yellow / gold foliage stealing the show.

**It is best planted in fairly sheltered locations in full sun to bring out the vivid yellow foliage to the full.**

| 20 | | |
|---|---|---|
| Mature height: 20m | Shape of mature tree | Evergreen trees |

Kelly Gold differs from the species in having foliage which flushes gold before hardening to a yellow green. Like its parent it is easily identified from all the other Cedars due to its trailing leader and this large, evergreen conifer has a gently pendulous habit. It thrives on most soils though is not happy on waterlogged ground.

● Telephone 01353 720 748  ● www.barcham.co.uk  ● Fax 01353 723 060

# CEDRUS libani
## *Cedar of Lebanon*

Few trees, deciduous or evergreen, can compare with the beauty and elegance of a mature Cedar of Lebanon. Some think it is its own species or that it is a geographical sub species of Cedrus atlantica but either way there is little to choose between them. It won the Award of Garden Merit in 2002.

One of the most majestic of all trees and extensively planted as part of the enduring landscape of some of our grandest stately homes and estates. It is slower growing than the Atlas Cedar, conical when young before assuming the flat topped and tiered habit of maturity. Introduced to England around the time of the Civil War in the mid 1640s, it has large, barrel shaped cones and green or grey / green foliage. It thrives on most soils though does not appreciate wet ground.

Mature height:
20m+

Shape of
mature tree

Evergreen
trees

So impressive are the trees at the Cedars Conservancy Parks in Lebanon it was put forward as a candidate for the new listing of the Seven Wonders of the World. The variety 'Brevifolia' is sometimes listed and is a native of Cyprus.

Cedar of Lebanon has been very important to many civilizations including the ancient Egyptians who used its resin for mummification. Sawdust from the tree has also been present in many of the Pharaohs tombs. However its range has been sadly depleted over time as its timber has been too highly prized by humankind and much of the original forests are no more.

# CELTIS australis
## *Nettle Tree*

The wood of the Nettle Tree was once used to produce charcoal. A native of Southern Europe and North Africa, it has been grown in the UK since the 16th century and is used commonly as a verge or street tree in the Mediterranean as it is tolerant of both reflected heat and salt laden air.

Related to the elms, this small to medium tree has broad, lanceolate, rough leaves. It has a broad crown and smooth trunk. It is widely planted for roadside shade in southern Europe, and the bark has been used to produce a yellow dye. Good for avenue and park plantings, where it will withstand much pollution, and is also very good close to coasts. It thrives on most soils, including very dry ones.

Mature height: 10-15m    Shape of mature tree    Coastal sites

---

# CELTIS occidentalis
## *Hackberry*

**Although part of the Elm family, this tree is immune to Dutch elm disease. A native of North America, it makes a medium sized tree in the UK.**

It is a vigorous tree with arching stems that support large heart shaped soft green leaves. At maturity the bark becomes corky and rough and the tree produces small black fruits in profusion. A great tree for parkland and estates, it thrives on most soils. In the States on deep fertile soils they have been known to reach 35 metres in height and live for over 200 years.

Mature height: 10-15m    Shape of mature tree    Parkland trees

---

# CERCIDIPHYLLUM japonicum
## *Katsura Tree/Candyfloss Tree*

The Katsura Tree was introduced from the Far East in the early 1880s and won the Award of Garden Merit in 2002. Often thought of as a small ornamental tree I stumbled across one in Rutland a few years ago that must have been over 20 metres tall. It is best grown away from frost pockets or exposed windy sites as new foliage can scorch before they harden.

Sometimes mistaken for Cercis siliquastrum, this has smaller leaves. It is sensational both in spring with emerging coppery green leaves and autumn when the foliage turns yellow or pink whilst exuding a fragrant scent reminiscent of burnt sugar. A great choice for gardens and parks, doing best on deep, fertile soils.

Mature height: 15-20m    Shape of mature tree    Garden trees

• Telephone 01353 720 748   • www.barcham.co.uk   • Fax 01353 723 060

# CERCIS canadensis
# Forest Pansy

*North American Redbud*

A native of South Eastern Canada and Eastern USA, it is not as free flowering as Cercis siliquastrum but this clone makes up for it by its stunning deep red / purple leaf colour. Grown and supplied as either a standard tree or multi-stemmed specimen, we rate this as one of the best purple foliaged trees on the market. It won the Award of Garden Merit in 2002.

It makes a small tree of rounded habit and is ideal for sunny urban gardens and courtyards. It does best in free draining soils and like Cercis siliquastrum is slow to root so we recommend stakes to be retained for the first three years after planting. Flowers are a light pink and the autumn brings a luminescent red quality to the senescing leaves. A wonderful small garden tree.

Like many trees with distinctly coloured leaves, full sun is needed to keep the leaf tone vivid. Too much shade dulls the leaf to a dark green. This tree is also keen on hot summer temperatures to encourage growth so south facing locations are a must for this clone.

**5|10**
Mature height: 5-10m

Shape of mature tree

Red/purple foliage

# CERCIS siliquastrum
## *Judas Tree*

A most beautiful tree despite its association with Judas Iscariot. Introduced in the 16th century, it won the Award of Garden Merit in 2002. It is very slow to root so is one of the few trees we recommend to stake for up to three years after planting. A native of the Eastern Mediterranean, it is a must for any garden large enough to give it justice!

A stunning sight in May when clusters of rosy-lilac, pea-like flowers wreathe the wood, sometimes springing direct from mature branches and even from the trunk. These are followed by purple tinted seed pods from July onwards.

Mature height: 5-10m

Shape of mature tree

Flowering trees

It slowly forms a well rounded tree, and is perfect for sunny urban gardens and courtyards, tolerating dry conditions well. It thrives on most soils, including very dry ones.

● Telephone 01353 720 748   ● www.barcham.co.uk   ● Fax 01353 723 060

# CHAMAECYPARIS lawsoniana
# Columnaris Glauca

Raised in Boskoop, Holland, in the 1940s, this small and narrow conical tree has enormous garden or parkland appeal.

**Densely arranged ascending branches carry flattened foliage sprays which are greenish blue and pure blue on the growing tips. Many conifer clones of this type have come and gone over the years but this one has passed the test of time and remains one of the best blue conifers around for restricted areas. It thrives best on most soils, though it is not happy on wet ground.**

Mature height: 5-10m | Shape of mature tree | Evergreen trees

# CHAMAECYPARIS lawsoniana
# Stardust

Introduced from Holland in the 1960s, this outstanding yellow variety won the Award of Garden Merit in 2002.

Densely arranged branches carry flattened foliage sprays which are golden yellow and bronze on the growing tips. It is columnar in habit so suitable for most gardens and parks. It tolerates most soils although, like most Chamaecyparis, soils prone to water logging should be avoided.

Mature height: 5-10m | Shape of mature tree | Evergreen trees

# CHAMAECYPARIS lawsoniana
# Yvonne

**I liken this to the golden equivalent of 'columnaris Glauca'. Surely one of the most stunning golden uprights on the market, this clone is ideal for gardens and parks.**

Ascending branches support green / gold sprays of foliage that are luminescent gold on the growing tips. Like others of its group, it dislikes water logged ground and thrives on well drained sunny sites. The overall habit is columnar so it is a great plant for restricted places.

Mature height: 5-10m | Shape of mature tree | Evergreen trees

# CHITALPA tashkentensis Summer Bells

A recent hybrid between Chilopsis and Catalpa. Original work on these pairings was undertaken at the Uzbek Academy of Science in Tashkent, Uzbekistan, in the 1960s before being introduced internationally in the mid 1970s.

This small hybrid with a rounded form initiates flower bud in June / July which open to produce an abundant display of frilly pink flowers with yellow throats for the rest of the summer. Best planted on well drained soils in full sun with protection from strong winds. Ideal for sheltered gardens and streets.

| 5\|7 Mature height: 5-7m | Shape of mature tree | Flowering trees |

# CLERODENDRUM trichotomum

Brought from China and Japan and in cultivation since the 1880s this highly interesting tree won the Royal Horticultural Society's First Class Certificate in 1893.

It is a small tree, but a strong grower. White, strongly fragrant flowers, enclosed in maroon calyces, appear in August and September. They are followed by bright blue berries and a glorious display of autumn foliage of luminescent reds to yellows. It thrives on most soils but is best to avoid wet and exposed sites. Although very hardy in England, it would be put to the test if subjected to colder and more northerly aspects of the UK.

| 5\|7 Mature height: 5-7m | Shape of mature tree | Flowering trees |

Telephone 01353 720 748 • www.barcham.co.uk • Fax 01353 723 060

# CORDYLINE australis
## *Cabbage Tree*

Introduced from New Zealand in 1823, this sun lover won the Award of Garden Merit in 2002 and 1953. Best planted in Southern England, it produces small, creamy white, flowers in early summer when mature.

A very architectural tree, it grows as either a single trunk specimen or a multi-trunk plant. Large and ascending green sword like leaves give it a Yucca like appearance. It develops into a small evergreen tree and is tolerant of most well drained soils.

Mature height: 5m

Shape of mature tree

Garden trees

# CORNUS controversa
## *Wedding Cake Tree*

This wonderful introduction from China and Japan has been grown in the UK since the 1880s and won the Award of Merit in 1984. One of the best specimens to look out for is at the Bath Botanic Garden. Wonderfully architectural, its striking form draws the eye through any garden.

A small to medium tree with a conical habit, its common name relates to the layered effect of its branches. Broad clusters of creamy flowers cover the branches in May. Small, black fruits develop in autumn as the foliage turns to a rich purple-red. Excellent for parks and gardens, it thrives on most soils.

Mature height: 5-7m

Shape of mature tree

Garden trees

# CORNUS controversa Variegata

Introduced in the 1890s this variegated version of the Wedding Cake Tree is a sight to behold when seen at its full potential. It is far from easy, hence the fact you hardly ever see one, but planted in a sheltered spot with plenty of care and time it is uniquely beautiful.

Layered branches take shape from an early age but are characterised by the striking white to yellow margin of the otherwise green leaves. A winner of the Award of Garden Merit in 2002 it is far more sedate than its parent listed previously but well worth the wait.

Mature height:
3-5m

Shape of
mature tree

Variegated
trees

This dainty tree is best planted in dappled shade as full sun can scorch the sensitive leaves. It is particularly effective when used as an underplant beneath the open canopies of mature trees.

# CORNUS Eddie's White Wonder

This is a cross between Cornus florida and Cornus nuttallii which has won a host of awards including the First Class Certificate, the Cory Cup, and the Award of Garden Merit. It has fallen out of favour in America, where it was raised, for not being as hardy as first thought but it is absolutely fine in the more temperate UK.

We supply this superb garden plant as a maturing bush which produces large white flower heads in the spring. It thrives on most soils but we do not recommend planting on alkaline or waterlogged ground. It forms a compact small garden tree at maturity.

Mature height:
3-5m

Shape of
mature tree

Garden
trees

● Telephone 01353 720 748  ● www.barcham.co.uk  ● Fax 01353 723 060

# CORNUS kousa China Girl

Introduced in the late 1970s and selected in Holland, this variety has large bracts, great autumn colour and good sized fruits. Plants as small as 40-60cm are capable of setting flower buds making this an ideal garden tree that exhibits lots of interest.

Flowers are borne in abundance in early spring and the foliage turns vivid colours by autumn. Supplied as a maturing bushy shrub, it will eventually make a small tree. Cornus kousa types do not thrive in alkaline soils, they just linger. Best only to plant on ground with a ph less than 7 and to avoid waterlogged or compacted soils.

Mature height:
3-5m

Shape of
mature tree

Garden
trees

# CORNUS kousa Chinensis

Perhaps the most reliable of all flowering dogwoods. Bean reckoned the fruits were both sweet and edible but I think he was getting carried away by the glamour of the plant as believe me there are better things to eat.

**This small, open tree flowers in June, the white bracts turning from soft green to white to pink and lining the upper sides of almost horizontal, slender branches. It goes on to give pink, arbutus-like berries and rich bronze and crimson autumn leaves. It prefers acid and well drained soils.**

Mature height:
5-7m

Shape of
mature tree

Garden
trees

# CORNUS kousa Milky Way

Selected from a seedbed in Ohio USA in the 1960s, this highly floriferous clone is considered to be one of the very best of its type.

We grow this as a multi-stem bush rather than as a standard tree as the flowers are so plentiful it is nice to view them from ground level upwards. Like all kousa types it does not thrive on alkaline soils. Ideal for small gardens or for centre pieces on estates.

Mature height:
3-5m

Shape of
mature tree

Garden
trees

# CORNUS kousa Stella Pink

It is not easy to grow a kousa type as a standard form but this delightful small garden tree lends itself to be grown with a single trunk and a dominant central leader. Raised by Dr Elwin Orton at Rutgers University, New Jersey in the late 1980s for its vigour and disease resistance.

The glossy leaves of this rounded tree turn a rich crimson-bronze in autumn. Remarkable for its pink, star-shaped bracts. Autumn colour is lovely, with hints of orange and reds. Very good for parks and gardens, but will not thrive on alkaline soils and waterlogged or compacted ground.

| 5|10 | | |
| Mature height: 5-10m | Shape of mature tree | Garden trees |

# CORNUS mas

*Cornelian Cherry*

**Introduced in the late 1890s, the Cornelian Cherry gives a very long period of interest. A native of central and southern Europe, it won the Award of Merit in 1929.**

From February onwards when the small, yellow flowers appear on the bare twigs this Cornus puts on a great display. The bright red, cherry-like fruits are edible, and the leaves turn a delightful reddish purple in autumn. Often grown as a multi-stem bush, we have managed to raise ours on a single stem to 1.8m with a well balanced and compact crown. A very good choice for parks. It thrives on most soils.

| 5|10 | | | |
| Mature height: 5-10m | Shape of mature tree | Multistem | Flowering trees |

# CORNUS mas Variegata

First recorded in 1838 this stunning small tree won the Award of Garden Merit in 2002 and 1981. One of the best examples of a mature specimen can be seen in the Bath Botanic Garden, fairly close to the Malus trilobata!

The leaves are beautifully white margined and the variety, like its parent plant, is free fruiting. It prefers a sheltered spot and is best kept away from intense direct sunlight where it can scorch; a dappled shade would be perfect. It is so striking it is always the first tree you notice in a collection.

| 3|5 | | |
| Mature height: 3-5m | Shape of mature tree | Variegated trees |

● Telephone 01353 720 748 ● www.barcham.co.uk ● Fax 01353 723 060

# CORYLUS avellana

## *Hazel*

The squirrel's favourite, also known as the cobnut or Filbert, this is our native Hazel. We supplied our neighbour with 34 plants in 2007 and this has now made a fantastic instant hedge that you can view when you visit Barcham.

A small tree with a rounded habit, it looks particularly striking in the early spring when it is adorned with its long yellow "lambs tail" catkins. The nuts in autumn aren't bad either! A very good choice for gardens, parks and woodlands. We supply this tree as a multi-stemmed coppiced specimen that makes a great under plant for a woodland or instant infill within a hedgerow.

Quick to grow, we recommend a five year cycle of coppicing down to only a few inches above ground level. This can be done in February / March after the catkins finish and although you will sacrifice any fruiting potential for that year, you will end up with a more bushy and vibrant plant as a result.

315

Mature height: 3-5m

Shape of mature tree

Native trees

# CORYLUS avellana Contorta
## *Corkscrew Hazel*

This Hazel is also known as Harry Lauder's Walking Stick, after the Scottish music hall performer who had a trademark "twisted" walking stick. At maturity it looks like a quirky bonsai and the best example of this I have seen is in my mother's garden in Surrey.

A very small and slow growing tree that has strangely twisted and contorted branches which create a dense and rounded habit. It is believed to have been discovered in a Gloucestershire hedgerow in the 1860s. A real curiosity for parks and gardens. Small twiggy branches can be sympathetically removed and used to add interest to seasonal floral displays.

Mature height: 3-5m | Shape of mature tree | Garden trees

# CORYLUS avellana Zellernus

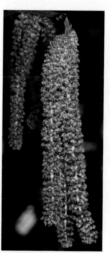

**Also known as Red Filbert, this is a great improvement on Corylus maxima Purpurea. I have one in my garden that I coppice on a four yearly rotation to encourage the young red foliage to shine out in the spring.**

This rounded and rather rare tree looks spectacular in spring when it is festooned with pink catkins set against its rich purple foliage that turns dark green by early summer. Delicious red Filbert nuts are an added bonus in the autumn. It is most attractive in gardens or parks and particularly effective when randomly scattered into a hedgerow.

As with Common Hazel, coppicing every five years invigorates the plant and keeps it bushy from ground level upwards.

Mature height: 3-5m | Shape of mature tree | Edible nuts

Telephone 01353 720 748 • www.barcham.co.uk • Fax 01353 723 060

# CORYLUS colurna
## *Turkish Hazel*

A splendid and truly beautiful tree from South East Europe and West Asia that was introduced in 1582 and won the Award of Garden Merit in 2002. It is large, imposing and rather columnar when young before broadening to a symmetrical pyramid on maturity. Notable for its roughly textured, corky bark, it produces long, yellow catkins in early spring and clusters of fringed nuts in autumn.

Turkish Hazel is a superb choice for parkland and avenue planting, and it will tolerate paved areas. It thrives in all soils, including chalky and clay soils and is now used in cities as a substitute for Lime to combat the problem of aphid drop on cars and pavements.

| 20+ | Shape of mature tree | Avenue trees |
|---|---|---|
| Mature height: 20m+ | | |

# COTONEASTER
# Cornubia

Raised at the famous Exbury Gardens in the early 1930s this versatile small tree won the Award of Garden Merit in 2002 and 1933 as well as the First Class Certificate in 1936. It is a particularly useful tree for stilted semi evergreen screening in small gardens where privacy is needed.

Sometimes categorized under Cotoneaster x watereri and elsewhere said to be a cultivar of Cotoneaster frigidus, we list it as Cornubia. It is a small to medium, semi-evergreen tree which bears large red berries in abundance in the autumn. Usually grown as a shrub, we grow it as tree with a 1.8m clear stem and find it develops a nicely rounded crown at maturity. It does well in most soils.

| 5|7 | Shape of mature tree | Garden trees |
|---|---|---|
| Mature height: 5-7m | | |

# CRATAEGUS x grignonensis

This is a hybrid of Crataegus mexicana and has been in cultivation since the mid 1870s. In southern parts of Britain it can be considered as a semi evergreen making it a useful small tree for dappled screening.

This small tree of rounded habit is late both in flowering and in the ripening of its big, scarlet fruits. A good choice for urban and coastal planting it is also tolerant of air pollution. It does well in most soils, both wet and dry. The leaves are sometimes retained throughout winter if the weather is mild enough.

Mature height: 5-10m

Shape of mature tree

Garden trees

# CRATAEGUS laevigata
# Paul's Scarlet

This small hawthorn tree was a sport of Crataegus Rosea Flore Plena found in a Herefordshire garden in the 1850s. Probably the most popular of thorns on the market, it won both the First Class Certificate in 1858 and the Award of Garden Merit in 2002.

**It becomes smothered in double, red flowers in May which are all the more stunning as the spring flowering cherries have finished their display by then.**

Mature height: 5-10m

Shape of mature tree

Garden trees

As root development can be rather slow, we recommend moderate pruning in the first few years after planting so that good anchorage is achieved. A good choice for urban and coastal planting, it is tolerant of air pollution. It does well in most soils, including very dry and wet soils.

● Telephone 01353 720 748  ● www.barcham.co.uk  ● Fax 01353 723 060

# CRATAEGUS x lavalleei
## *Hybrid CockspurThorn*

**A small hawthorn tree which produces a dense crown of thorn clad branches that give rise to its trademark rounded habit at maturity. Originating back to the 1870s this fine tree won the Award of Garden Merit in 2002 and 1924.**

The large white flowers are followed by orange haws, which are retained for most of the winter. The oval, glossy, leathery leaves persist until December, colouring from red through to yellow. As it is only slightly thorny, it makes a better street tree than most other hawthorns. A good choice for urban and coastal planting, it is tolerant of air pollution. It does well in most soils, including very dry and wet soils.

Mature height: 5-10m

Shape of mature tree

Urban trees

# CRATAEGUS x lavalleei Carrièrei

A hawthorn of garden origin, dating from around 1870, that won the Award of Garden Merit in both 1924 and 2002. This clone is particularly resistant against rust.

It makes a small, densely headed tree with glossy, deep green foliage which lasts through to December. The orange-red haws are also long lasting, often right through winter, and they contrast well with the dark foliage. A good choice for urban and coastal planting, it is also tolerant of air pollution. It does well in most soils, including very dry and wet soils. Like many clonal variations it is difficult to tell apart from its parent variety.

Mature height: 5-10m

Shape of mature tree

Urban trees

# CRATAEGUS monogyna
## *Common Hawthorn*

Also known as Quickthorn or May, this small native hawthorn has many ancient associations and is most seen as hedgerow plants along the span of the UK. However we run it up to make a standard tree for specimen planting and it is without doubt one of our prettiest native trees.

The small white, fragrant flowers which appear in May and June are followed by small red fruits in abundance during autumn, providing much needed food for wild birds. A good choice for urban and coastal planting it is also tolerant of air pollution. It does well in most soils, including very dry and wet soils.

| 5\|10 | | |
|---|---|---|
| Mature height: 5-10m | Shape of mature tree | Native trees |

# CRATAEGUS monogyna
## Alboplena

**This small tree is very similar in most respects to Crataegus monogyna, but has double white flowers. It is worth remembering that while hawthorns are often seen as hedgerow trees, they also make fine garden trees – and this is one of the best.**

A good choice for urban and coastal planting it is also tolerant of air pollution. It does well in most soils, including very dry and wet soils. Originating back to the 1770s, many classify this as Crataegus laevigata Alba Plena but the differences are too close to call and as both are derivatives of native trees we choose to place it here.

| 5\|10 | | |
|---|---|---|
| Mature height: 5-10m | Shape of mature tree | Garden trees |

# CRATAEGUS monogyna Stricta

A tough and durable hawthorn, ideal for exposed situations. Its dark green leaves and very regular habit make this a favourite for urban planners where space is at a premium. It thinks nothing of reflected heat and light bouncing off windows and pavements making it a very versatile native variation of the traditional hedgerow parent.

Very different from other hawthorns in that it has a columnar habit with tightly ascending branches, making it a very good prospect for both streets and small gardens. It is also a good choice for coastal planting and tolerant of salt laden winds. It does well on most ground, including very dry and wet soils.

| 5\|10 | | |
|---|---|---|
| Mature height: 5-10m | Shape of mature tree | Narrow trees |

Telephone 01353 720 748  •  www.barcham.co.uk  •  Fax 01353 723 060

# CRATAEGUS x prunifolia
## *Broad-leaved CockspurThorn*

This small hawthorn is thornier than most others and won the Award of Garden Merit in 2002. It has wonderful autumn colour and is a winter provider for birds feasting on its profuse red fruits. Sometimes referred to as Crataegus x persimilis, it is a hybrid between Crataegus crus galli and Crataegus macracantha and originates from Eastern America.

This small, compact, round-headed tree produces long sharp thorns along the span of its branches. The burnished, oval leaves, which turn a glorious red in autumn, are accompanied by plentiful small, red fruits. A good choice for urban and coastal planting, it is also tolerant of air pollution. It does well on most ground, including very dry and wet soils.

5|10
Mature height: 5-10m

Shape of mature tree

Urban trees

# CRATAEGUS x prunifolia Splendens

A clonal selection of Crataegus prunifolia that is very similar to its parent in every way apart from its uniformity. Originating from Holland, it is ideal for both street verges and gardens and has all the inbuilt durability of its genera. It is a great tree for wildlife with birds especially benefitting from the abundant autumn crop of shiny red berries.

Wonderful red and golden autumn foliage is a striking feature of this small tree with a regular and rounded habit at maturity. It also has characteristic white flowers and shiny, leathery, oval leaves. A good choice for park and coastal planting it is also tolerant of air pollution. It does well in most soils, including very dry and wet soils. Be sure to crown lift the stem to 2 metres over time to keep the thorns out of reach.

| 5\|10 Mature height: 5-10m | Shape of mature tree | Garden trees |

This much underused tree requires little maintenance after establishment and is seldom seen in Garden Centres where 'Paul Scarlet' seems to dominate. It is a small tree of ultimate size that makes a wonderful garden tree offering spring flower, lovely berry colour and great autumnal colour.

● Telephone 01353 720 748 ● www.barcham.co.uk ● Fax 01353 723 060

# CRYPTOMERIA japonica Elegans
## *Japanese Cedar*

Introduced by Thomas Lobb from Japan in 1854, this beautiful bushy conifer eventually makes a small tree at maturity. Its wonderful texture and feathery appearance makes you want to touch it!

**3|7**
Mature height: 3-7m

Shape of mature tree

Evergreen trees

## *Japanese Cedar*

Evergreen feathery foliage turns bronze in winter and at this point many despair and make a phone call to us but this is all part of the annual show it performs. It tends to grow as wide as it does high but reacts well to pruning if necessary. It thrives in most soils though does not like water logged ground. It is such an unusual foliage plant that it provides wonderful contrast within a garden and many gardeners struggle to indentify it quite simply as it looks like nothing else!

# CUPRESSUS arizonica Glauca

**A selection of the Smooth Arizona Cypress, this striking conifer is a native of South Eastern America. I have seen this grown as a hedging conifer in Southern France and it positively glitters when it is filmed by a morning dew.**

This medium to large evergreen conifer forms a dense, pyramidal habit at maturity with very distinctive rich brown bark that peels in flakes. Its deeply fragrant blue foliage is particularly attractive and its rounded cones swell in spring. Tolerant of air pollution, it is good for urban plantings and large gardens. It thrives on most soils.

**15|20**
Mature height: 15-20m

Shape of mature tree

Evergreen trees

# CUPRESSUS macrocarpa Goldcrest

A British-bred form of the Monterey Cypress, raised by Treseder of Truro in the late 1940s, this spectacular conifer won the Award of Garden Merit in 2002. Its yellow colour is so vivid that it provides wonderful contrast to a dark landscape.

A medium size tree, and therefore much smaller than the species, Goldcrest has a narrow, columnar habit and rich yellow, feathery foliage. Certainly one of the best of its colour, it remains dense and compact. Very good for avenues, gardens and parks. It thrives on most soils.

| 10\|15 | | |
|---|---|---|
| Mature height: 10-15m | Shape of mature tree | Evergreen trees |

# CUPRESSUS sempervirens
*Italian Cypress*

**The Italian Cypress is surely one of the most beautiful and evocative trees in the world! If you ever get out to Tuscany or Umbria you will be well and truly hooked on this wonderful conifer.**

The cypress of Mediterranean antiquity, and widely used in the middle Ages to make chests because its pleasant smelling timber helped to keep clothes sweet. In Britain it is best to avoid cold, exposed sites for this architecturally columnar beauty, but it is a splendid choice for urban plantings and courtyard gardens. It does best in rich, fertile soils.

| 10\|15 | | |
|---|---|---|
| Mature height: 10-15m | Shape of mature tree | Narrow trees |

● Telephone 01353 720 748 ● www.barcham.co.uk ● Fax 01353 723 060

# CUPRESSOCYPARIS leylandii
## *Leyland Cypress*

Love it or loathe it, the Leyland Cypress is Europe's fastest growing conifer. It is a cross between Chamaecyparis nootkatensis and Cupressus macrocarpa and is probably Britain's most well known tree.

**Unbeatable for screening, but rather too tall for most small gardens, this is a tall, handsome tree with a dense, columnar habit. Single specimens and plantings in avenues show off this rather unfairly maligned conifer to best advantage. Very good for coastal plantings, where it tolerates salt laden winds. It does well in most soils, including chalk.**

Mature height: 20m+

Shape of mature tree

Hedging trees

# CUPRESSOCYPARIS leylandii Castlewellan
## *Golden Leyland Cypress*

The Golden Leyland Cypress is often considered more amenable than the green leaved form though in Ireland it has been so overplanted there is a lobby for making future plantings illegal! However, this is not the trees fault and it remains an excellent choice for evergreen hedging.

Slower growing and rather more useful for hedging than its green parent, it is also rather smaller and the pale golden foliage adds to the interest of this attractive seedling, which was raised in County Down in the early 1960s. Very good for coastal plantings, where it tolerates salt laden winds. It does well in most soils, including chalk.

Mature height: 10-15m

Shape of mature tree

Hedging trees

# DAVIDIA involucrata
## *Handkerchief Tree, Dove Tree*

Whether known as the Handkerchief Tree or Dove Tree, it is well-named and much-loved. Discovered in China by Père David in 1869 and introduced in 1904, this is one of the great beauties of the plant world. The variety 'Vilmoriniana' is often specified but there is little or nothing to choose between this and its parent.

Its common names derive from the large white bracts which appear in May. These are followed by large, oval fruits in autumn. Foliage and habit are similar to those of the lime. A medium to large tree, it is very good for parks and does best in a fairly sheltered position. On a historical note, it first flowered in England in 1911 on Vieitch's Coombe Wood Nursery. It thrives best on deep fertile soil.

I first saw this tree at Kew's sister garden Wakehurst Place in Sussex. It was in full flower and even though the tree was still relatively young it was mighty impressive.

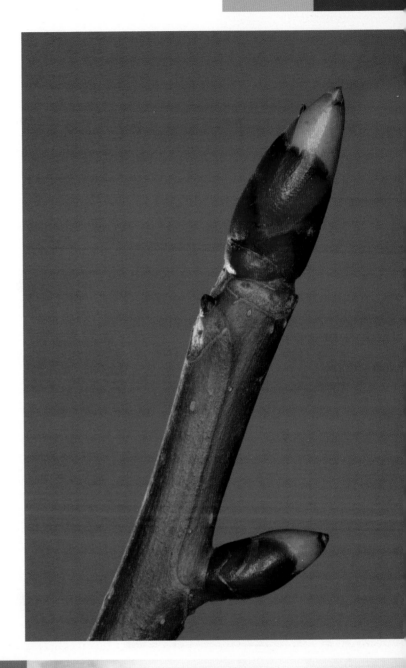

Mature height: 10-15m

Shape of mature tree

Flowering trees

From our experience of growing this tree in the Fens it is clear that it thrives best on less exposed sites and is best pruned lightly in the summer rather than when it is dormant in the winter. Growing tips can frost off if subjected to icy winds and invariably the best specimens are seen nestled away in a comfy sheltered spot.

# DIOSPYROS lotus

## *Date Palm*

This hardy Date Palm, a close relative of the persimmon, has been in cultivation since the 1590s. A good choice for arboretums and plant enthusiasts who like catching out their peers on tree identification.

Deciduous and native to China, in the UK it makes a fairly small tree with shiny, green, tapered foliage. Female plants produce purple or yellow fruits, which resemble small tomatoes. It does best in fertile, well drained soils.

Mature height: 10-15m | Shape of mature tree | Edible fruits

# DIOSPYROS kaki

## *Japanese Persimmon*

Introduced from China in 1796, this small tree has been grown in the Far East for hundreds of years for its edible egg shaped yellow orange fruits.

In the UK it is grown more for its superb autumn colour display of its large vibrant leaves which turn orange, yellow, red and purple before they fall. Fruits are set from new season's growth but only achieve full potential in the UK in hot long summers. Flowers appear in May / June.

Mature height: 5-7m | Shape of mature tree | Edible fruits

# ELAEAGNUS angustifolia Caspica

## *Oleaster, Russian Olive*

The Oleaster is also known as "Quicksilver". A native of Southern Europe, this tough striking evergreen won the Award of Garden Merit in 2002 and 1978. It is thought to be a cross between Elaeagnus commutata and Elaeagnus angustifolia.

This small tree is remarkable for its exceptionally silvery, narrow foliage. It does well in most soils, except shallow chalk, and appreciates a position in full sun. Recommended for gardens and where space is limited, but it is prone to suckering.

Mature height: 10-15m | Shape of mature tree | Evergreen trees

● Telephone 01353 720 748 ● www.barcham.co.uk ● Fax 01353 723 060

# EUCALYPTUS
## debeuzevillei

*Juonama Snow Gum*

One of the hardiest of all Eucalyptus, being a native of the high mountains of south east Australia, it is also one of the most dramatic. As a point of interest, grab hold of its leaves on a hot summer's day and you will immediately notice how cold they are. This is true of all Eucalyptus; they are nature's air conditioning units!

A medium sized tree of broadly pyramidal form, it has a beautiful white patchwork trunk and thick lanceolate evergreen leaves. A superb specimen for both parks and gardens, it produces stunning and unexpected dandelion clock like flowers from mid summer straight from its branches. It thrives on most soils.

**10|15**

Mature height:
10-15m

Shape of
mature tree

Bark
interest

This wonderfully dramatic tree has so much year round interest that it should be considered more often for large gardens and municipal parks and verges. Its foliage provides great contrast within the landscape and always seems to draw the eye. Interestingly, Eucalyptus does not have a dormancy period and carries on growing, very slowly, even in the winter months.

# EUCALYPTUS gunnii

*Cider Gum*

This Gum is a native of the highlands of Tasmania and Australia and was introduced to the UK in the mid 1850s. A winner of the Award of Garden Merit in both 2002 and 1950, this striking tree is also well suited to being grown as a multi-stemmed coppiced specimen.

A very well known Eucalyptus – and a very hardy one – this large, broadly pyramidal tree has smooth grey-pink to red-brown bark. The young leaves are grey-green and glaucous providing a wonderful contrast to gardens and municipal landscapes. For those florists amongst you, the foliage is particularly good to compliment cut flower arrangements. It thrives on most soils.

When faced with selecting Eucalyptus never be tempted to go for the biggest and probably most pot bound. A strange physiology comes into play in that when Eucalyptus roots spiral they tend to carry on that way and are prone to falling over through lack of anchorage over time. This is a particular problem exasperated by trees grown in black pots.

| 15\|20 | | |
|---|---|---|
| Mature height: 15-20m | Shape of mature tree | Garden trees |

# EUCALYPTUS niphophila

*Snow Gum*

A well known and lovely Eucalyptus with attractive grey, green and cream patchwork bark. A winner of the Award of Garden Merit in 2002.

Its leaves are narrow and grey-green when matured and it is well suited as a specimen tree to provide lovely soft contrast in parks and large gardens. It is slower growing than the more common Eucalyptus gunnii but it forms such a pleasing architectural shape of superb patchwork stems it is hard to beat. If the decision was forced upon me I would choose this as a multi-stem and Eucalyptus debeuzevillei as a single stem as they are both superb trees!

| 10\|15 | | |
|---|---|---|
| Mature height: 10-15m | Shape of mature tree | Garden trees |

● Telephone 01353 720 748  ● www.barcham.co.uk  ● Fax 01353 723 060

# EUODIA hupehensis

A small genus and a must for any collector with an arboretum. Others list this as Tetradium daniellii but it is the same tree, caught up in a botanical debate to confuse everyone. Native of China and Korea, it was introduced into the UK in 1905 and won the First Class Certificate in 1976.

Its compound leaves and panicles of small white flowers make this an attractive specimen tree that is excellent for shallow chalk soils. Bright red fruits are borne on female trees in the autumn. The flowers are characterised by lovely yellow anthers and are pleasingly fragrant. Autumn colour is a pale yellow.

| Mature height: 15-20m | Shape of mature tree | Parkland trees |

# EUONYMOUS europaeus
# Red Cascade

A good choice even on chalky soils. This wonderful garden tree won the Award of Garden Merit in both 1949 and 2002. It has so much interest from September onwards that it is one of my favourite trees for a small garden. Named 'Red Caps' in America, this clone was selected by the University of Nebraska for the richness in colour of its fruits.

This small, arching tree produces an abundance of rosy red fruits which open up to reveal vivid orange seed cases. The foliage display in the autumn is fantastic with green leaves turning into rich red foliage by November. It is one of the very best forms for gardens, parks and restricted areas. It thrives on most soils though avoid waterlogged ground.

| Mature height: 3-5m | Shape of mature tree | Garden trees |

# FAGUS sylvatica

## *Common Beech*

One of the most majestic of our native trees, the Common Beech can become very large with its low branched habit. My favourite specimen is in a private garden in North Luffenham, Rutland and what a beauty it is!

It has a wide range of uses – in woodland, parkland and in broad verge plantings – and few trees can surpass its rich, copper autumn foliage. Beech thrives just about anywhere other than exposed and coastal locations. As it is shallow rooted, under planting is not recommended. It does well in most reasonably fertile, well drained soils, except heavy clay or light sand.

Beech tends to favour more temperate climates and is difficult to establish when faced with extreme heat and drought. With this in mind avoid planting in paved or tarmac areas where reflected heat and light makes Beech suffer.

20+

Mature height:
20m+

Shape of
mature tree

Parkland
trees

● Telephone 01353 720 748  ● www.barcham.co.uk  ● Fax 01353 723 060

# FAGUS sylvatica Asplenifolia

## *Cut-leaved Beech*

The common name of Cut-leaved Beech comes from the deeply serrated and long leaves of this beautiful tree of medium height. Introduced in the early 1800s, this wonderful specimen tree won the Award of Garden Merit in 2002.

It is pyramidal in its early years, but is eventually capable of becoming as wide as it is tall. A lovely choice for parkland where its cut leaves gives magnificent contrast. Beech thrives just about anywhere other than exposed and coastal locations. As it is shallow rooted, under planting is not recommended. It does well in most reasonably fertile, well drained soils, except heavy clay or light sand.

Sometimes referred to at Fagus sylvatica Heterophylla, it is in fact the same thing. There are few cut leaf trees that last the test of time but this is surely one of the best. The key for planting is to give it the space it merits at maturity, a minimum ten metre radius.

10|15 Mature height: 10-15m · Shape of mature tree · Parkland trees

# FAGUS sylvatica Dawyck

*Fastigiate Beech*

The Fastigiate Beech – a rather ugly name for a rather beautiful tree! Originating in Dawyck, Scotland, in the mid 1800s, this architectural beauty won the Award of Garden Merit in 2002. There are some wonderful specimens planted by some of the university colleges in Cambridge.

This medium to large tree has a columnar habit and is a very good choice for both wide verges and specimen plantings in parks. Even when mature, it is seldom more than 3m wide. Beech thrives just about anywhere other than exposed and coastal locations. As it is shallow rooted, under planting is not recommended.

Mature height: 15-20m | Shape of mature tree | Narrow trees

# FAGUS sylvatica Dawyck Gold

A golden-leaved form of the Fastigiate Beech. It is thought to be a seedling cross between Fagus sylvatica Dawyck and Fagus sylvatica Zlatia and was raised by JRP van Hoey-Smith in 1969. A real architectural beauty and winner of the Award of Garden Merit in 2002.

A fairly large, columnar tree, which looks good from spring right through to autumn. In spring the leaves are golden yellow, turning pale green in summer before reverting to a golden yellow in autumn. It looks especially attractive planted against a dark background and is good as a specimen in parks and as a verge tree.

Beech thrives just about anywhere other than exposed and coastal locations. As it is shallow rooted, under planting is not recommended. It does well in most reasonably fertile, well drained soils, except heavy clay or light sand.

Mature height: 15-20m | Shape of mature tree | Narrow trees

## FAGUS sylvatica Dawyck Purple

A Fastigiate Beech with stunning dark foliage. Raised from the same seed source as Dawyck Gold in 1969 from a Dawyck at Trompenburg Arboretum near Rotterdam in Holland, it won the Award of Garden Merit in both 1973 and 2002. It remains a rare but stunning architectural specimen tree.

Mature height: 15-20m | Shape of mature tree | Narrow trees

A little narrower than Dawyck Gold but not quite as dense. It makes a splendid tree for parks and verges and has striking, deep purple foliage. Beech thrives just about anywhere other than exposed and coastal locations. As it is shallow rooted, under planting is not recommended. It does well in most reasonably fertile, well drained soils, except heavy clay or light sand.

## FAGUS sylvatica Pendula

### *Weeping Beech*

The Weeping Beech is a wonderful choice as a specimen in parks and large estates. Introduced in the mid 1830s, this stately tree won the Award of Garden Merit in 2002. Mature specimens have been known to weep to the ground and then layer up from the soil to weep again when a new trunk is formed. With this in mind they can get pretty big over the long term!

This medium to large tree has a majestic crown with large, horizontal and pendulous branches which gives the tree a unique architectural beauty. Beech thrives just about anywhere other than exposed and coastal locations.

Mature height: 10-15m | Shape of mature tree | Parkland trees

# FAGUS sylvatica Purpurea
*Purple Beech*

The Purple Beech is one of our most beautiful trees. A superb tree for creating contrast in a parkland or large garden as the darkness of the foliage draws the eye through the landscape. With this in mind it is useful to plant this on the perimeter of your area as if it is too close in view you never notice beyond it.

This large, rather conical tree with its dark purple leaves is sometimes wrongly referred to as "Copper Beech", which is seed grown and variable in leaf colour.

Mature height: 20m+

Shape of mature tree

Red/purple foliage

This cultivar has a much deeper purple leaf, and is a tree of great beauty and majesty. It makes a magnificent subject planted as a specimen in parks and large estates. Beech thrives just about anywhere other than exposed and coastal locations. As it is shallow rooted, under planting is not recommended. It does well in most reasonably fertile, well drained soils, except heavy clay or light sand.

● Telephone 01353 720 748   ● www.barcham.co.uk   ● Fax 01353 723 060

# FAGUS sylvatica Rohanii

Thought to be a cross between Fagus sylvatica Quercifolia and Purpurea, this extremely pretty tree is relatively rare but highly prized. Introduced in the mid 1890s, we only ever have a few to sell every year so if you wanted one for your collection it would be best to reserve in good time!

Perhaps best described as a purple leaved form of Fagus sylvatica Asplenifolia, this slow growing, small, pyramidal tree is perfect for parks and large open spaces. Beech thrives just about anywhere other than exposed and coastal locations. As it is shallow rooted, under planting is not recommended. It does well in most reasonably fertile, well drained soils, except heavy clay or light sand.

Mature height: 5-7m   Shape of mature tree   Parkland trees

# FAGUS sylvatica Roseomarginata

One of the smallest Beeches and one which does best in a sunny, rather sheltered position. Introduced in the late 1880s its availability restricts it to arboretum planting so it is rarely seen. However, spot a good one and you will not forget it! Others list it as Fagus sylvatica Purpurea Tricolor.

The purple leaves of this small to medium, rounded tree, which only seldom reaches 15m, have attractive pink edges. The width of these margins is variable and the foliage sometimes displays pink-white stripes. It does best in a sunny, sheltered position, and is good for parks and woodland plantings.

Mature height: 5-10m   Shape of mature tree   Parkland trees

# FEIJOA sellowiana

This small tree is native of Brazil and Uruguay and was discovered by Friedrich Sellow in 1819. Just to confuse everyone its name has recently been changed to Acca sellowiana but we are still classifying as we always have done just to be rebellious!

Evergreen grey-green leaves, white felted beneath, do best in a warm sheltered position and large pods are sometimes produced in hot summers from flowers that have crimson and white petals. Only for south facing, hot and sheltered sites. It is lovely for both being evergreen and producing such highly prized ornamental flowers. It thrives on most soils.

Mature height: 5-10m   Shape of mature tree   Evergreen trees

# FICUS carica
## *Common Fig*

A native of Western Asia, this well known fruiting tree was introduced into the UK in the early 16th century. It is remarkably resistant to pest and disease and can be grown for either its foliage or fruit as both add ornamental interest to a south facing garden.

It makes a small and elegant tree with a rounded habit that does best in a warm, sheltered position, producing its green fruits by early August. Perfect for gardens or where space is restricted and often grown up against south facing walls to maximize fruiting potential.

Mature height: 3-5m    Shape of mature tree    Edible fruits

# FRAXINUS americana Autumn Purple

A superb selection that is very popular for municipal plantings in the USA. White Ash was introduced into the UK in 1724 but this clone is really worthy of note for its magnificent autumn colour display and robust branch structure that is far superior to the problematic Fraxinus Raywood.

A fast growing conical tree, Autumn Purple's dark green leaves turn reddish-purple in autumn before falling. Being Ash, it is very robust, establishing on made up ground as well as tolerating harsh urban conditions. At a young age the trunk is a smooth dark green. Ideal for large gardens, central reservations and wide verges.

Mature height: 15-20m    Shape of mature tree    Autumn colour

● Telephone 01353 720 748 ● www.barcham.co.uk ● Fax 01353 723 060

**Barcham**

# FRAXINUS angustifolia Raywood

This ash cultivar was introduced to Britain from Australia in the mid 1920s. Referred to by many as oxycarpa rather than angustifolia it won the Award of Garden Merit in 2002 and 1978. However, in my opinion Fraxinus americana Autumn Purple is a far safer bet due to its structural strength.

A fast growing ash of medium height and with a dense, upright, oval and relatively compact habit. It tolerates drier soils than Common Ash and its dark green leaves turn wine red in the autumn. This is a good choice for avenue and street plantings, and it bears soil compaction well. Its Achilles heel is the lack of strength of its branch unions which make it a mechanically weak tree and prone to collapsing over time.

**10|15**
Mature height: 10-15m

Shape of mature tree

Autumn colour

# FRAXINUS excelsior

*Common Ash*

This very tough native tree is well known for its timber uses. It is easily recognized when dormant as its buds are black. Late to leaf and early to fall, this is probably our toughest native tree.

It is more variable in habit to the variety Westhofs Glory so is often overlooked for avenue planting where uniformity is required. Ash is fast growing and produces vast quantities of fertile seed that can annoy gardeners. Best suited for parkland and highway verges. It thrives on most soils, including calcareous, and will tolerate windswept, exposed sites, coastal locations and air pollution.

**15|20**
Mature height: 15-20m

Shape of mature tree

Native trees

# FRAXINUS excelsior Altena

Introduced by the Forestry Commission in the mid 1940s, this cultivar of the Common Ash is an improved form, well suited to urban plantings. It tends to retain its central leader for many years more than common Ash, so giving it more structural strength.

A medium to large tree of pyramidal habit, at maturity it is difficult to tell apart from the species. We recommend it for avenue and street planting. It thrives in most soils and will tolerate windswept, exposed sites, coastal locations and air pollution.

Mature height: 15-20m

Shape of mature tree

Urban trees

# FRAXINUS excelsior Diversifolia
*One-leaved Ash*

The One-leaved Ash is a fast-growing tree which has been in cultivation since the late 1780s. It is not easily recognisable as an Ash when it is in leaf but look out for the tell tale black buds on dormant shoots to identify it.

Ideal for verge plantings, even by the busiest roads. I have seen this tree smothered with the soot of urban car pollution and it was still thriving! This large ash of pyramidal form is surely one of the most amenable of all trees – a real tough customer.

Mature height: 20m+

Shape of mature tree

Urban trees

# FRAXINUS excelsior Jaspidea
*Golden Ash*

The Golden Ash looks particularly beautiful in winter. Introduced in the late 1870s in won the Award of Garden Merit in 2002. Often referred to as 'Aurea', it is quite a different clone being far more vigorous and able to withstand the rigours of an urban environment.

This makes a large tree with a broad, pyramidal crown if the leader is retained. Like most ashes, it is fast growing and its twiggy branches stand out as golden in winter, preceded by stunning yellow autumn foliage. A good choice for parks and verges. It thrives in most soils and will tolerate windswept, exposed sites, coastal locations and air pollution.

Mature height: 15-20m

Shape of mature tree

Parkland trees

● Telephone 01353 720 748 ● www.barcham.co.uk ● Fax 01353 723 060

# FRAXINUS excelsior Pendula

## *Weeping Ash*

The Weeping Ash makes a fine specimen tree in a park or large garden. Dating back to the 1700s, there are several fine examples of this architectural weeping tree in the UK but as most were planted in the Victorian era they are mostly restricted to country houses or estates.

It always looks unimpressive as a nursery tree and needs several years' worth of growth to define its wonderful weeping shape. It thrives in most soils and will tolerate windswept, exposed sites, coastal locations and air pollution.

Mature height: 10-15m    Shape of mature tree    Parkland trees

# FRAXINUS excelsior Westhofs Glory

Much used for municipal planting in Europe, this clone originates back to the mid 1950s and won the Award of Garden Merit in 2002. It is a fast growing and large cultivar that has a narrow habit when young, spreading to become broadly oval as it matures. Very good for avenues, its healthy looking, glossy green leaves are quite late to open in spring. It thrives in most soils and will tolerate windswept, exposed sites, coastal locations and air pollution.

The desire for uniformity is high so most nurseries offer Westhofs Glory as a substitute for the common Ash which grows in a more irregular pattern. When we grow a batch of common Ash, after four years they would be a mix of 8-10cm girth to 12-14cm girth with a corresponding height differential. This is down to the seed all varying slightly in genetic makeup. A batch of Westhofs Glory that is vegetatively propagated and budded onto an ash rootstock, would all achieve 10-12cm girth over the same period with very little height difference, satisfying clients expectations.

Mature height: 20m+    Shape of mature tree    Urban trees

# FRAXINUS ornus

*Manna Ash, Flowering Ash*

The Manna Ash or Flowering Ash has been grown in Britain since before 1700. A sweet sap, known as manna, is extracted from the stems to make a laxative. A native of Southern Europe and South West Asia, it won the Award of Garden Merit in 2002.

Rather slow growing for an Ash, this eventually makes a rounded tree of medium height, producing plenty of creamy white, fragrant blossoms in late spring. It also provides excellent autumn colour when the foliage turns from yellow to red and orange. It does best on drier, calcareous and sandy, loamy soils and is particularly well suited to urban planting.

Mature height: 10-15m

Shape of mature tree

Flowering trees

# FRAXINUS ornus Arie Peters

One of the loveliest of the Flowering Ash cultivars, producing 10-15cm panicles evenly distributed throughout the crown during the growing season.

A medium tree which is very upright when young, but spreads to become broadly oval later in its life. It produces a mass of creamy, fragrant blooms in late spring that can sometimes continue until late in the summer. It also has good autumnal foliage tones. It thrives best on drier, calcareous and sandy, loamy soils.

Mature height: 10-15m

Shape of mature tree

Flowering trees

● Telephone 01353 720 748 ● www.barcham.co.uk ● Fax 01353 723 060

# FRAXINUS ornus Louisa Lady

This cultivar of the Flowering Ash gives spectacular autumn colour – much richer than that of the species. Fraxinus ornus varieties represent a far better bet that Fraxinus Raywood in that they are stronger in structure and Louisa Lady even matches the autumn colour display.

Mature height: 15-20m | Shape of mature tree | Autumn colour

A medium to large cultivar which has a uniformly broad pyramidal crown when mature that produces a mass of fragrant, creamy white flowers in spring. It thrives best on drier, calcareous and sandy, loamy soils. Best suited for large gardens, verges and central reservations.

# FRAXINUS ornus Meczek

This Flowering Ash is the perfect choice where space is limited. Often referred to as a lollipop tree, it would not occur naturally in this form but provides a purpose for city planners when a site cannot accommodate a conventional choice.

Brought from Hungary in the early 1980s, this top worked, small tree has a fine, rounded habit, and is slow growing. Recommended as a street and avenue tree, it is very good in most restricted areas, and has most attractive, shiny, dark green leaves. It thrives best on drier, calcareous and sandy, loamy soils.

Mature height: 5-7m | Shape of mature tree | Urban trees

# FRAXINUS ornus Obelisk

As its name suggests, this Flowering Ash has a narrow, columnar habit, ideal for restricted urban areas and smaller sized gardens. I have seen this planted along a small street in London and they have gone down a treat and been warmly welcomed by the residents.

An excellent choice for streets and avenues, this medium cultivar stands up well to paving and soil compaction. It retains its tight, columnar habit well and produces an abundance of flowers in spring. It thrives best on drier, calcareous and sandy, loamy soils.

Mature height: 10-15m | Shape of mature tree | Narrow trees

# FRAXINUS pennsylvanica Summit

An American selection of the Red Ash or, confusingly as it is also known, the Green Ash. Introduced from trials in Minnesota in 1957, there is some debate as to whether it is male or female but from what I have heard seed is not produced on mature trees.

The uniformity of this fast growing, medium to large tree, with ascending branches which form a broadly conical, well balanced crown, make it a superb choice for avenue plantings. Its green glossy leaves turn a beautiful golden yellow in autumn. It thrives in most environments making it a very versatile and tough urban tree.

Mature height: 15-20m | Shape of mature tree | Parkland trees

● Telephone 01353 720 748 ● www.barcham.co.uk ● Fax 01353 723 060

# GINKGO biloba

## *Maidenhair Tree*

Very common about 200 million years ago, this marvellous gymnosperm is making a comeback as an urban tree due to its no nonsense toughness. As it survived the radiation and devastation that wiped out 90% of all life when the comet fell to end the reign of the dinosaurs, it can cope well with traffic exhaust as well as reflected heat and light in our urban environments! Reintroduced into the UK from prehistoric times in 1754.

**This large, conical tree remains relatively narrow if the central dominant leader is retained. It is a good choice for parks and avenues, tolerating paved areas well.**

It has a deep root system, and curious, fan shaped leaves. Female plants fruit after 35 years or so and it is not possible to determine the gender until this event. We are boosting numbers of male clones, listed next, which are more expensive to produce but solve the fruiting dilemma.

**20+**
Mature height: 20m+

Shape of mature tree

Urban trees

# GINKGO biloba Lakeview

This male Scanlon introduction develops a compact pyramidal habit that is well suited for urban planting as it requires little maintenance so long as the well defined leader is left uninterrupted. There are good examples of this clone on the A47 planted on the way in and way out of Leicester.

Particularly useful for narrow city streets, this clone is well suited to deal with the reflected heat and light that bounces off pavement and buildings. It produces a great display of vivid yellow autumn colour and we should have them coming through to saleable production by 2014/15.

| 15\|20 | | |
| --- | --- | --- |
| Mature height: 15-20m | Shape of mature tree | Urban trees |

# GINKGO biloba Mayfield

This male clone was selected in Ohio in the late 1940s. Notable for its wonderful shape at maturity, it is the ginkgo equivalent of the Lombardy poplar. Autumn colour is a vivid yellow.

A great choice for an urban tree, it requires very little maintenance so long as the central leader is well defined and not interrupted. We should have this coming through into saleable production by 2012/13.

| 10\|15 | | |
| --- | --- | --- |
| Mature height: 10-15m | Shape of mature tree | Urban trees |

# GINKGO biloba Nanum

Top worked on Ginkgo biloba stem at 2m this spherical dwarfing shrub form makes as ideal little tree on sites that are too restricted to accommodate a more conventional choice.

Particularly useful for narrow city streets, this clone is well suited to deal with the reflected heat and light that bounces off pavement and buildings. It also copes with urban pollution making this clone a useful addition to the Ginkgo range.

| 4\|6 | | |
| --- | --- | --- |
| Mature height: 4-6 m | Shape of mature tree | Urban trees |

● Telephone 01353 720 748 ● www.barcham.co.uk ● Fax 01353 723 060

# GINKGO biloba Saratoga

**This handsome broadly pyramidal male clone retains a distinctive central leader and was introduced by the Saratoga Horticultural Foundation, California, in the mid 1950s. A tough and easily maintained urban tree that we have coming on line for sale for 2010/11.**

It has a wonderfully rich yellow autumn colour that stands out brilliantly against any setting. Otherwise, it is just the same as seedling Ginkgo with the notable difference of being guaranteed not to set fruit at maturity.

| 15\|20 | | |
|---|---|---|
| Mature height: 15-20m | Shape of mature tree | Urban trees |

# GINKGO biloba Tremonia

A superb male clone making a narrowly compact crown at maturity. Raised as a seedling in Dortmund Botanic Garden in 1930 by the late Dr G Krussmann.

Dramatic yellow autumn colour is another striking feature of this great urban clone that requires little maintenance once planted so long as its well defined leader is left uninterrupted. We will have this in saleable production by 2013/14.

| 15\|20 | | |
|---|---|---|
| Mature height: 15-20m | Shape of mature tree | Urban trees |

# GINKGO biloba Princeton Sentry

Raised by the famous but now sadly out of business Princeton Nursery in New Jersey. In our opinion this is the best of the upright forms but also the most difficult to produce hence its price tag over seedling Ginkgo!

A wonderful maintenance free choice for the urban environment, the only thing holding back this male clone is its availability. Slow to grow, we should have them coming through in decent volume by 2015. It is very similar to another Princeton introduction, Ginkgo biloba Magyar.

| 20+ | | |
|---|---|---|
| Mature height: 20m+ | Shape of mature tree | Urban trees |

G

# GLEDITSIA
## triacanthos
### *Honey Locust*

**A wonderful choice for heavily polluted environments prone to vandalism. Introduced from America in 1700, its seed pods hold a sticky sweet resin from which it derives its common name.**

This large, oval and rather elegant tree has leaves which resemble fronds. When mature, it looks most striking with its shiny, long seed pods. A good choice for parks and industrial areas, it does well in most soils. Be careful on handling this tree as it is very thorny!

Mature height: 20m+ — Shape of mature tree — Parkland trees

# GLEDITSIA triacanthos
# Inermis

### *Thornless Common Honey Locust*

For those tree surgeons among you this is a far better bet than seedling Gleditsia triacanthos for climbing and pruning as you haven't got to contend with the numerous vicious 3-5cm thorns.

Otherwise, it has the same attributes as the preceding listing and makes a useful choice for hard built up areas or a graceful inclusion for parkland.

Mature height: 15-20m — Shape of mature tree — Urban trees

Telephone 01353 720 748 • www.barcham.co.uk • Fax 01353 723 060

# GLEDITSIA triacanthos Sunburst

Although originally from moist and even swampy areas, the Honey Locust does well in much drier and free draining soils. Introduced in the mid 1950s it won the Award of Garden Merit in 2002. It is one of the best yellow foliaged trees on the market.

15|20
Mature height:
15-20m

Shape of
mature tree

Yellow
foliage

This medium to large cultivar has the advantage of being thornless. It has a rounded, rather spreading form and its yellow foliage, which appears late, is retained for most of the summer. We recommend it as a very good substitute for the more brittle Robinia pseudoacacia Frisia.

# GYMNOCLADUS dioica

*Kentucky Coffee Tree*

The Kentucky Coffee Tree is surely one of the most handsome of all trees. The seeds were used as a substitute for coffee beans by the early settlers in North America but are thought to be poisonous if not roasted first. The exact introduction date is vague but it is thought to have been planted in the UK since the 1750s.

This slow growing tree of medium to large size has large, compound leaves, which are pink tinged in spring and clear yellow in autumn. The young twigs are pale grey, almost white, and particularly noticeable in winter. A wonderful choice for parks.

15|20
Mature height:
15-20m

Shape of
mature tree

Parkland
trees

# HAMAMELIS x intermedia Arnold Promise

*Witch Hazel*

Raised and introduced by the Arnold Arboretum in the USA, this clone is internationally recognised as being one of the best of the yellow flowering Witch Hazels.

The original plant in the States is about 7 metres high and wide. It produces magnificent clear yellow flowers contrasting against red inners that last sometimes as long as two months without fading. It is all the more beautiful for being winter flowering.

Mature height: 3-5m

Shape of mature tree

Autumn colour

# HIBISCUS syriacus Cultivars

This genus was introduced from China and India in the 1600s and remains an exotic favourite with gardeners. Many varieties have emerged over this time and we major on clones that make a standard tree with a 1.8m clear stem which are suitable for either garden specimens or street planting. Given a position of full sun and a good summer the large trumpet sized flowers adorn the trees from August to October making this one of the glamour genera of our range. The great thing about Hibiscus is that it is at its best when most of the flowering interest in the garden has gone. It is tolerant of most soils but may suffer on ground prone to water logging.

Mature height: 3-5m

Shape of mature tree

Flowering trees

● Telephone 01353 720 748   ●   www.barcham.co.uk   ●   Fax 01353 723 060

# HIBISCUS syriacus Ardens

Introduced around 1873, 'Ardens' has pale purple double flowers with a deeper mauve throat. It is a fairly upright variety that broadens slightly with age.

Mature height: 3-5m  |  Shape of mature tree  |  Flowering trees

# HIBISCUS syriacus Duc de Brabant

Deep rose purple double flowers grace this cultivar by August and it was first seen in the UK in the early 1870s.

Mature height: 3-5m  |  Shape of mature tree  |  Flowering trees

# HIBISCUS syriacus Hamabo

This clone was introduced about 1935 and is widely regarded as one of the best cultivars. It produces large single pale blush flowers with a crimson eye.

Mature height: 3-5m  |  Shape of mature tree  |  Flowering trees

H

# HIBISCUS syriacus Lavender Lady

This prolific bloomer is smothered with light blue / lavender double flowers when in full swing. This can bring the garden back to life after other flowering plants have finished their displays.

Mature height: 3-5m    Shape of mature tree    Flowering trees

# HIBISCUS syriacus Morning Star

This dainty semi double white has a deep red throat. Like many of this range, it is best planted close to the house, south facing, so the flowers can be in constant view and enjoyed by all.

Mature height: 3-5m    Shape of mature tree    Flowering trees

# HIBISCUS syriacus Oiseau Bleu

This old French variety produces a wonderful display of single sky blue flowers with small red throats. Also known as 'Blue Bird', it was introduced in the late 1950s and won the Award of Merit in 1965 and the updated Award of Garden Merit in 2002.

Mature height: 3-5m    Shape of mature tree    Flowering trees

Barcham

# HIBISCUS syriacus Red Heart

A wonderful variety that has large white flowers with a striking red eye. Introduced around 1973, it won the Award of Garden Merit in 2002.

| | | |
|---|---|---|
| 3\|5 | Shape of | Flowering |
| Mature height: 3-5m | mature tree | trees |

# HIBISCUS syriacus Woodbridge

Vivid rose pink single large flowers with carmine centres give this clone a truly exotic appeal. Introduced about 1928 it has won both the Award of Garden Merit in 2002 and the Award of Merit in 1937.

| | | |
|---|---|---|
| 3\|5 | Shape of | Flowering |
| Mature height: 3-5m | mature tree | trees |

# HIBISCUS syriacus William R Smith

Beautiful pure white single flowers make this one of my personal favourites. Introduced around 1916 it won the Award of Garden Merit in 2002.

| | | |
|---|---|---|
| 3\|5 | Shape of | Flowering |
| Mature height: 3-5m | mature tree | trees |

# ILEX x altaclerensis Golden King

One of the very best golden variegated hollies. It was derived from a cutting of Ilex x Hendersonii in Edinburgh in 1884. It won the First Class Certificate in 1898 and the Award of Garden Merit in 2002.

Tolerant of coastal conditions and air pollution, this medium, slow growing tree of pyramidal form has vivid golden margins to its virtually spineless leaves. Very good for gardens, female, with reddish-brown fruits.

| 5\|10 | | |
|---|---|---|
| Mature height: 5-10m | Shape of mature tree | Variegated foliage |

# ILEX aquifolium

*Common Holly*

**One of the most evocative and best loved of all trees; the Common Holly is beautiful in its simplicity and brings cheer at the darkest time of year. It is very tolerant of shade and prefers well drained soils.**

This native of Britain is a small, conical, evergreen tree which provides year-round interest, but is particularly attractive in autumn and winter. Great for gardens, it only retains its spiky leaves within the first ten feet of height in the tree, as after this point it suffers no predation so has no need for a thorny defence.

| 5\|10 | | |
|---|---|---|
| Mature height: 5-10m | Shape of mature tree | Native trees |

● Telephone 01353 720 748 ● www.barcham.co.uk ● Fax 01353 723 060

# ILEX aquifolium Alaska

**A great clone of common Holly with spiky, dark, glossy foliage. We grow this variety as a single stemmed full standard tree ideal for either specimen planting or for spot screening. Female.**

The dark evergreen foliage contrasts well with the vivid red berries that are produced in the autumn. It retains an upright pyramidal habit and is a useful tree for screening in gardens. Tolerant of shade and prefers well drained soils.

Mature height: 5-10m | Shape of mature tree | Evergreen trees

# ILEX aquifolium Argentea Marginata

*Broad-leaved Silver Holly*

This lovely clone won the Award of Garden Merit in 2002. Ideal for hedging or specimen planting, it prefers free draining soils and is tolerant of shade.

It is a most dramatic small tree with spiny leaves, edged with white, and plenty of berries for winter and wildlife interest. Young growth is tinged pink. Slow growing and female.

Mature height: 5-10m | Shape of mature tree | Variegated trees

# ILEX aquifolium J C Van Tol

This self pollinating Holly is in our opinion one of the best green leaved bush Hollies on the market. It won the Award of Garden Merit in 2002 and for those of you who like making up Christmas wreaths this is the clone for you!

This vigorous cultivar has very dark, shiny, almost spineless leaves and a good show of autumn berries. It remains a small tree with a good pyramidal form. Excellent for gardens, it prefers well draining soils and is tolerant of shade.

Mature height: 5-10m | Shape of mature tree | Evergreen trees

# ILEX aquifolium Pyramidalis

This fast growing Holly has apically dominant growth and is self pollinating. A winner of the Award of Merit in 1989 and the Award of Garden Merit in 2002, it makes a great evergreen tree for gardens where space is restricted.

This clone has smooth leaves and retails a pyramidal shape if the leader is retained. Plenty of red berries in the autumn compliment its bright green evergreen leaves. It is tolerant of shade and prefers free draining soils.

**5|10**
Mature height:
5-10m

Shape of
mature tree

Evergreen
trees

# ILEX castaneifolia
*Sweet Chestnut-leaved Holly*

A great favourite at Barcham, this female Holly is a vigorous grower and won the Award of Garden Merit in 2002. It is a form of Ilex x keohneana and is thought to be of French origin.

Its thick green leaves are large and resemble the shape and form of Castanea sativa from which it derives its name. Its good apical dominance produces a medium to large tree of conical habit. Red berries are produced in abundance in the autumn and it is tolerant of shade. Like all hollies it will thrive on most soils so long as they are well drained.

**5|10**
Mature height:
5-10m

Shape of
mature tree

Privacy raised
screening

# ILEX x Nellie Stevens

**This clone was derived from a seed source collected by Ms Stevens in 1900 from the US National Arboretum. It is a hybrid between Ilex aquifolium and Ilex cornuta and is exceptional for its vigour and readiness to make a small single stemmed tree.**

Smooth dark glossy leaves contrast well with the orange-red berries in autumn and we supply this cone as a feathered bush or as a clear stemmed standard at semi mature. Ideal for spot screening and it tolerates most free draining soils. Female.

**5|10**
Mature height:
5-10m

Shape of
mature tree

Privacy raised
screening

# JUGLANS nigra

## *Black Walnut*

**Introduced from native central and eastern America into Europe in 1629, this fast growing tree won the Award of Garden Merit in 2002. The national US champion stands at 44 metres high by 47 metres wide in Oregon so not one to be planted in restricted places.**

It makes a large tree with a broadly pyramidal crown and is a very good choice for parkland settings. It produces an abundance of nuts over a long period, but they are rather difficult to extract from their very hard shells. Rough barked from a young age so easily distinguished from the smooth barked Juglans regia. It grows on most soils but thrives on deep loam.

Mature height: 20m+

Shape of mature tree

Edible nuts

# JUGLANS regia

## *Common Walnut*

A native of South Eastern Europe, Himalaya and China, this well known tree is highly prized for its timber. It makes a splendid and stately subject for parkland and avenue plantings, developing a broad crown at maturity and preferring full sun. Thought to have been in cultivation in the UK since Roman times.

Slow growing and of medium to large stature, this rounded Walnut has delightfully aromatic young foliage, from which a wine can be made, followed by a good crop of delicious nuts. Smooth barked when young, it thrives on most soils but does not favour waterlogged conditions.

Mature height: 15-20m

Shape of mature tree

Edible nuts

# JUNIPERUS communis Hibernica
*Irish Juniper*

Introduced in the late 1830s, this is an excellent choice of small conifer, ideal for gardens and large rockeries. It won the Award of Garden Merit in 2002.

Its slender and dense form imposes a sense of architectural formality to a garden and it requires little or no maintenance. It tolerates most soils but does not thrive on waterlogged ground.

| 5 | | |
|---|---|---|
| Mature height: 5m | Shape of mature tree | Narrow trees |

# KOELREUTERIA paniculata
*Pride of India*

**Also known as the Golden Rain Tree, this was introduced from China in the 1760s but it is also a native of Japan and Korea. It is a tougher tree than most credit.**

A most attractive, rounded tree of medium height, it deserves to be more widely grown as it has much to recommend it. The clusters of small yellow flowers which it produces in July and August are followed by lantern shaped fruits in the autumn. It does best in dry, calcareous soils and in a reasonably sunny position.

I have seen this tree thriving on a narrow soil strip of central reservation in south London taking all urban pollution can throw at it. For such a pretty tree it can tolerate locations where our native trees would soon succumb to failure.

| 5|10 | | |
|---|---|---|
| Mature height: 5-10m | Shape of mature tree | Flowering trees |

● Telephone 01353 720 748  ● www.barcham.co.uk  ● Fax 01353 723 060

# KOELREUTERIA paniculata Fastigiata

**A columnar form of Pride of India. Raised by Kew Gardens from seeds received in 1888 from Shanghai, this botanical oddity is a must for plant collectors.**

A good choice for restricted spaces and excellent as a specimen tree in a park. The clusters of small yellow flowers which it produces in July and August are followed by lantern shaped fruits in the autumn. It does best in dry, calcareous soils and in a reasonably sheltered position, such as an urban courtyard garden.

| Mature height: 5-10m | Shape of mature tree | Narrow trees |

# LABURNOCYTISUS Adamii

This remarkable tree, a graft chimaera, is thought to have been fluked when a nurseryman from M Adam nurseries near Paris in 1825 turned his attention to grafting purple flowered broom after finishing with Laburnum.

Whether intentional or not the result was extraordinary! The plant looks more like laburnum than anything else until it flowers when some branches bear the anticipated yellow flowers of Laburnum while others bear dense clusters of the purple flowered Cytisus. Just to confuse matters further most branches also produce intermediate flowers of coppery pink! There is a particularly good specimen at Kew gardens.

It tends to thrive on most soils though dislikes water logged conditions. As it is so rare it is best planted as an individual specimen in a tree collection.

| Mature height: 5-10m | Shape of mature tree | Flowering trees |

# LABURNUM vulgare

A well known and stunning spring performer. Also known as Laburnum anagyroides it is native of central and southern Europe and was introduced into the UK in the early 1560s. The coppiced / multi-stemmed form of common Laburnum is the most effective way of appreciating the floral display of yellow racemes in the spring.

The seed set from the flowers are poisonous so care should be taken with children if planting in a garden. Laburnum take a little longer to establish than other trees so keep staked for at least two years after planting. It thrives on most soils.

The seeds are produced in pea like pods and are black and shiny when ripe which may entice an unwary victim but in truth this occurrence is extremely rare and it is my belief that quite a quantity has to be consumed for a fatal dose.

| 5\|10 | | |
| --- | --- | --- |
| Mature height: 5-10m | Shape of mature tree | Flowering trees |

● Telephone 01353 720 748  ● www.barcham.co.uk  ● Fax 01353 723 060

# LABURNUM x watereri Vossii

A most floriferous cultivar that won the Award of Garden Merit in 2002. Selected in Holland late in the 19th century, it has remained very popular over the years and is readily seen in gardens up and down the UK.

This small tree produces a wealth of yellow racemes up to 50cm long in spring. All parts of the plant are highly poisonous as it contains an alkaloid called cytosine. It thrives on most soils and is particularly effective when grown as an arching avenue.

One of the very best examples of this is at Bodnant Gardens in North Wales where the abundant flowers droop down above you and fill the air with their fragrance.

Much is made of its black seeds being fatal if eaten and rightly so, but occurrences of laburnum poisoning are extremely rare. Educating children to keep away from this genus is the key.

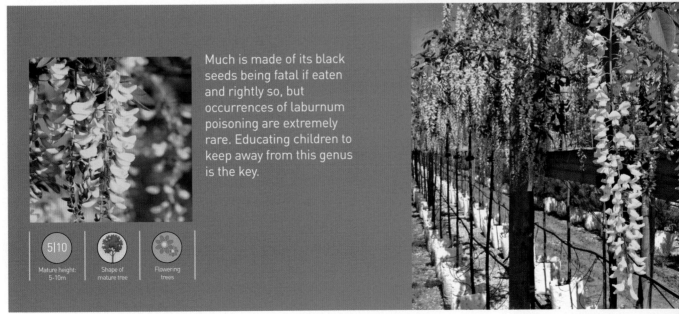

| 5|10 | | |
|---|---|---|
| Mature height: 5-10m | Shape of mature tree | Flowering trees |

# LAGERSTROEMIA
## indica Rosea

*Crape Myrtle*

This selection of the Crape Myrtle is best grown in south facing and sheltered locations. Native of both Korea and China, it was introduced into the UK in 1759 and won the Award of Garden Merit in both 1924 and 2002.

A beautiful small tree with a rounded, somewhat flat-topped growth. The bark is most attractive, being mottled with grey and pink, while the small, dark green leaves turn flame red in autumn. The deep rose pink flowers, with their crimped petals, are borne late summer but are only initiated after warm summers.

Much has been made of climate change over the last decade and I find it interesting that we have routinely been able to get our Lagerstroemia to flower in recent years. When I first started growing trees in the late 1980s this tree was treated as half hardy and flowers were not even considered.

**5|10**

Mature height: 5-10m

Shape of mature tree

Flowering trees

# LAGERSTROEMIA indica Violacea

Similar in every way to the cultivar 'Rosea' this lovely small tree produces clusters of violet flowers from late August onwards so long as the summer gives enough heat. Flowers are often initiated in even the dullest summers but do not fully emerge unless we have decent weather in September and October. It is well worth taking the risk!

A beautiful small tree with a rounded, somewhat flat-topped growth. The bark is most attractive, being mottled with grey and pink, while the small, dark green leaves turn flame red in autumn.

| 5\|10 | | |
|---|---|---|
| Mature height: 5-10m | Shape of mature tree | Flowering trees |

# LARIX x decidua

*Common Larch*

**A lovely deciduous conifer and underused in amenity plantings. Being coniferous it has very good apical dominance, so retaining a lovely pyramidal habit through to maturity. Not a native tree but introduced into the UK in the early 1600s. It won the Award of Garden Merit in 2002.**

Ideal for verges, as a specimen tree for parkland, or for woodlands, its crown is slender and conical when young. At maturity the older branches droop. Glorious green foliage heralds the spring and the autumn colour of yellow-orange provide good contrast. It thrives on most soils. We supplied some for the A47 coming into Leicester in 2001 and they are romping away!

| 20+ | | |
|---|---|---|
| Mature height: 20m+ | Shape of mature tree | Parkland trees |

● Telephone 01353 720 748 ● www.barcham.co.uk ● Fax 01353 723 060

# LARIX x eurolepis

## *Dunkeld Larch, Hybrid Larch*

Discovered at Dunkeld, Perthshire, around 1904, this hybrid is particularly robust and is a cross between Larix decidua and Larix kaempferi. In truth all the Larch we grow have very similar attributes and are difficult to distinguish. I would choose this cultivar for its toughness.

| 20+ | | |
|---|---|---|
| Mature height: 20m+ | Shape of mature tree | Parkland trees |

It is a large and fast growing tree with good timber and amenity value. Ideal for street verges or parkland, this deciduous conifer is, in my opinion, greatly underused. There is something primeval about Larch, a wonderful relic to an age before us.

# LARIX kaempferi

## *Japanese Larch*

This deciduous conifer was introduced from its native Japan in the early 1860s by the well known plant enthusiast JG Veitch. It thrives on most soils and is great for verges, parkland or large gardens.

A fast growing and large tree of conical form, the bright green leaves turn yellow in autumn. Its twiggy growth is tinged red, and when seen as a plantation against a setting sun in the winter the effect of this is quite dramatic.

| 20+ | | |
|---|---|---|
| Mature height: 20m+ | Shape of mature tree | Parkland trees |

# LAURUS nobilis

*Bay Laurel*

**We grow this as a clear stemmed full standard tree. A native of the Mediterranean, it was introduced in the early 1560s though it's foliage probably hit these shores a lot earlier when Julius Caesar visited with a wreath of it on his head! It won the Award of Garden Merit in 2002.**

A very useful evergreen tree that reacts well to pruning to form a dense pyramidal tree well suited for screening or specimen planting. The aromatic foliage can be added to bolognaise sauce for extra flavour. Suitable for most free draining soils. It prefers to be planted in areas of semi-shade and is also coastal tolerant.

Often considered as a half hardy plant when young, it proves to be particularly tough when older and combats the vagaries of UK winters very well. When it is used as a potted plant in a garden the soil volume may freeze in winter making it impossible for the plant to access water. Drought is the killer here, not hardiness.

Mature height:
5-10m

Shape of
mature tree

Garden
trees

Telephone 01353 720 748 ● www.barcham.co.uk ● Fax 01353 723 060

# LIGUSTRUM japonicum
## *Japanese Tree Privet*

Introduced in 1845 by PF von Siebold from its native Japan, this is often used as a stilted hedge above the fence line so is a favourite in urban gardens where privacy is needed. It can be planted very close to buildings without fear of subsidence and is compliant as such with the building regulation code. It is very useful in a small garden as its trunk below the fence line takes up little garden space.

**5|7**
Mature height: 5-7m

Shape of mature tree

Privacy raised screening

A small semi-evergreen tree, it is generally regarded as an evergreen in the south of England. It has a rounded habit, long, pointed leaves and white flowers, which are borne in autumn. Very good in restricted areas and it thrives on most soils.

# LIGUSTRUM lucidum
## Variegata

A variegated form of Chinese Privet and a good choice for urban settings. Sometimes listed as 'Superbum', it won the Award of Garden Merit in 2002. We grow this as a full standard so it is an ideal candidate for planting close to a fence line to provide screening cover over the fence height.

A most striking, top worked form with a rounded habit. A small semi-evergreen tree, it is generally regarded as an evergreen in the south of England. It has long, pointed gold margined leaves and white flowers, which are borne in autumn. Very good in restricted areas and it thrives on most soils.

| 5|7 | | |
|---|---|---|
| Mature height: 5-7m | Shape of mature tree | Privacy raised screening |

● Telephone 01353 720 748  ● www.barcham.co.uk  ● Fax 01353 723 060

# LIQUIDAMBAR
## acalycina

A fast growing form of Sweet Gum introduced from China in the 1980s. Its three lobed leaves and general habit are very similar to Liquidambar formosana but it is much hardier and it grows with a tough vigour. Unlike most other Sweet Gum clones, it is better known for its spring and summer foliage effect than its autumn colour.

| | | |
|---|---|---|
| 10\|15 | | |
| Mature height: 10-15m | Shape of mature tree | Parkland trees |

Of pyramidal form and medium height, it produces bronze-purple foliage that is retained with flushing new growth throughout the growing season. It turns to yellow in autumn and leaves are often retained until well into winter. Suitable for streets, avenues and parks, it does best in fertile, well drained soils. It does not thrive in chalky soils.

# LIQUIDAMBAR styraciflua
## *Sweet Gum*

**The Sweet Gum is one of the finest trees for autumn colour. Introduced from its native Eastern USA in the 17th century, it won the equivalent of the Award of Garden Merit in 1975.**

Sometimes confused with maple on account of its similar leaves, this makes a large tree with a broad, pyramidal crown if its central leader is retained. Its attractive, corky bark is a feature at all times of the year, but it is at its magnificent best in autumn when it simply seems to burn with crimson and gold. Suitable for streets, avenues and parks, it does best in fertile, well drained soils. It does not thrive in chalky soils.

| 20+ | | |
|---|---|---|
| Mature height: 20m+ | Shape of mature tree | Avenue trees |

# LIQUIDAMBAR styraciflua
# Lane Roberts

This sweet gum cultivar is particularly reliable in Britain and won the Award of Garden Merit in 2002. Like many of the styraciflua cultivars, the bark is smooth rather than corky. When planted en masse the autumn effect is both sensational and long lasting.

The autumn colour of the foliage is a highly dramatic dark crimson to red. A medium size tree, it has a tighter conical habit and larger leaves than the species. A good choice as a street or garden tree, it does best in fertile, well drained soils, but does not thrive in chalky soils.

| 10|15 | | |
|---|---|---|
| Mature height: 10-15m | Shape of mature tree | Garden trees |

Barcham

# LIQUIDAMBAR styraciflua Stella

This Sweet Gum with deeply cut star-like leaves resembles a semi dwarfing clone of Liquidambar Worplesdon. Prized for its autumn colour, this is a wonderful tree for a medium to large garden. Its bark is smooth rather than corky.

The bright green foliage of spring and summer turns from golden yellow through to crimson as autumn progresses. Stella is a medium to large tree of pyramidal habit; its leaves are similar to, but slightly smaller than, Worplesdon. Suitable for streets, avenues and parks, it does best in fertile, well drained soils. It does not thrive in chalky soils.

10|15
Mature height:
10-15m

Shape of
mature tree

Autumn
colour

# LIQUIDAMBAR styraciflua Thea

This lovely Sweet Gum is broad leaved and late to colour in the autumn, starting with the top third of the tree which turns a remarkable purple. A recent introduction, selected in the Netherlands.

Thea is in many respects similar to Lane Roberts, but as a medium to large tree, is a little taller. It has a good, conical form and distinctive purple foliage in the autumn. A good choice as a street or garden tree, it does best in fertile, well drained soils, but does not thrive in chalky soils.

15|20
Mature height:
15-20m

Shape of
mature tree

Autumn
colour

# LIQUIDAMBAR styraciflua Manon Variegata

This Sweet Gum is a must for those who like their variegated trees. The striking foliage is best in summer and can provide excellent contrast against a dark evergreen background.

This medium size cultivar, with its horizontal lateral branches, has a very regular, pyramidal form. It is of medium height and resistant to both pests and disease. Its blue-green foliage, with a creamy white margin, turns pink in autumn. Suitable for streets, avenues and parks, it does best in fertile, well drained soils. It does not thrive in chalky soils.

15|20
Mature height:
15-20m

Shape of
mature tree

Garden
trees

# LIQUIDAMBAR
## styraciflua
## Worplesdon

**Unlike most other Sweet Gums, this clone often bears fruit in British conditions. A winner of the Award of Garden Merit in both 1987 and 2002, this is our favoured clone of Liquidambar for both autumn colour and form. I have one thriving in my garden on a very thin and slightly alkaline soil.**

Its foliage is delightful and more deeply lobed than other clones and its pyramidal habit is both reliable and architecturally pleasing. However its real beauty lies in its autumn colour starting in September when some leaves turn yellow through to orange before falling but the outermost leaves gradually turn to magnificent claret red. A great tree for any urban aspect where space allows.

Mature height: 20m+

Shape of mature tree

Autumn colour

● Telephone 01353 720 748  ● www.barcham.co.uk  ● Fax 01353 723 060

# LIRIODENDRON tulipifera

## *Tulip Tree*

Introduced from America in the late 1680s this stately tree is known as Whitewood in North America, where the timber is widely used in house interiors. There are some tremendous specimens in the States that have grown to over 60 metres in height. As an aside, if you ever prune the young wood, take time to breathe in the sweetly fragrant sap.

**20+**

Mature height: 20m+

Shape of mature tree

Parkland trees

## *Tulip Tree*

A large and fast growing tree, it has a broad, pyramidal crown. The tulip shaped flowers, which appear only on older trees, are produced in June and July and are yellow-green with a band of orange at the base. It is deep rooted and wind resistant, and does well on most fertile soils. A splendid subject for parks and large gardens. Apparently, excellent honey is derived from bees harvesting its flowers.

● Telephone 01353 720 748 ● www.barcham.co.uk ● Fax 01353 723 060

# LIRIODENDRON tulipifera Aureomarginatum

This form of the Tulip Tree has yellow variegation to its leaves and was introduced in the early 1900s. The British champion I have heard is in Stourhead and stands at over 25 metres tall. The foliage is at its most striking in the spring.

Mature height: 10-15m | Shape of mature tree | Garden trees

Growing rather smaller than the species, this is a medium tree with a pyramidal habit. The bright yellow variegation tends to turn greenish-yellow by the end of the summer. It is deep rooted and wind resistant, and does well on most fertile soils. Lovely for parkland settings.

# LIRIODENDRON tulipifera Fastigiatum

This very upright form tends to flower earlier than its parent and we regularly see a decent floral display on 12-14cm girth crop. Like fastigiate hornbeam it can be prone to a bit of middle aged spread so allow for a bit more room around it at planting than you think.

Its stiffly ascending branches are very effective if kept as a feathered tree, eventually competing with the leader to become a fat tear drop shape at maturity. It is good as a specimen or as an avenue tree and thrives in most fertile soils.

Mature height: 10-15m | Shape of mature tree | Garden trees

# MAGNOLIA x brooklynensis Elizabeth

**Raised in New York by Eva Maria Sperbes in the 1970s, it is a cross between Magnolia acuminata and denudata. One of the finest yellows. The jury is still out on its ultimate shape and vigour as it is so recent an introduction.**

This lovely small conical tree produces clear, pale primrose-yellow cup shaped flowers in the spring that are nicely fragrant. The flowers tend to be a deeper yellow the cooler its position, but make sure it is well placed for spring viewing as its show can be breathtaking.

Mature height: 5-10m

Shape of mature tree

Garden trees

# MAGNOLIA chameleon

## Chang Hua

A very pretty cultivar that is known to flower three times in a single year in its native China. We grow this on a single stem to be raised as a standard specimen tree and its last flowering can be as late as the autumn.

The flower is beautifully upright, tulip shaped, and nicely fragrant. The outside of the flower is flushed pink, particularly at the base of the cup. Like all magnolias, give a newly planted tree no competition from other plants for the first couple of years to quicken establishment.

Mature height: 5-10m

Shape of mature tree

Flowering trees

# MAGNOLIA denudata

## Yulan

Introduced from China in 1789, this tree won the First Class Certificate in 1968 and won the Award of Garden Merit in 2002.

Fragrant pure white flowers emerge cup shaped in spring, opening with heavy duty petals. Fruits, seldom produced away from its native land, can be 10cm in length and turn rose red when ripe. This is a beautiful tree in flower, when the weather permits, but is rarely seen in the UK.

Mature height: 5-10m

Shape of mature tree

Flowering trees

● Telephone 01353 720 748   ● www.barcham.co.uk   ● Fax 01353 723 060

# MAGNOLIA grandiflora Gallissonière

This Magnolia was being grown in France prior to 1750 so is more in tune with European winters. It is difficult to tell apart from its parent and is now a popular choice for urban gardens in southern Britain.

A very hardy, evergreen clone, it produces large flowers, while the large, green leaves are tinted reddish brown underneath. It is of medium stature and broadly oval in habit. We offer it as a standard well-suited to urban planting.

Mature height: 10-15m    Shape of mature tree    Privacy raised screening

# MAGNOLIA Heaven Scent

**A member of the Swelte Brunettes Group of Magnolias this lovely variety won the Award of Garden Merit in 2002. We grow it as a standard tree with an oval crown that broadens at maturity.**

A superb small tree with heavily scented, rather narrow, cup shaped flowers in April. It has pale pink petals, flushed with a deeper pink towards the base, and a cerise stripe on the back. Ideal for sheltered urban gardens and parks.

Mature height: 5-10m    Shape of mature tree    Flowering trees

# MAGNOLIA kobus

Introduced in 1865 from Japan, this sturdy Magnolia is both very hardy and versatile. Unlike the other magnolias we supply, this only flowers at its full potential after about 15 years but as we supply them well over five years old it isn't too long to wait! In between time you will have a decent display rather than a sensational one.

We grow this medium size, round headed tree as a full standard, and recommend it for planting on verges and in parkland. It does well in most soils, including chalky ones. The very large, white flowers are produced as early as March and can reach up to 10cm across. This is definitely the best choice for neutral to high ph soils.

Mature height: 10-15m    Shape of mature tree    Flowering trees

# MAGNOLIA x loebneri Leonard Messel

**A chance cross between Magnolia kobus and Magnolia stellata Rosea, originating at Colonel Messel's Nymans garden in Sussex. Often sold as a shrub, we also grow this as a single stemmed small tree that would grace any garden.**

One of the prettiest and most delightful Magnolias, it produces abundant dainty white-lilac flowers in spring. It only makes a small tree so is perfect for a garden and it is reasonably lime tolerant.

As many as 12 to 15 petals adorn a single glorious flower and in the spring the tree is smothered with velvety cased buds waiting to burst. In my opinion this is the pick of 'garden' Magnolias and even the oblivious register this beauty when it is in full swing.

| Mature height: 3-5m | Shape of mature tree | Multi-stem | Garden trees |

Telephone 01353 720 748 • www.barcham.co.uk • Fax 01353 723 060

# MAGNOLIA x loebneri Merrill

An outstanding American selection, raised at the Arnold Arboretum, Boston, in the late 1930s and the winner of more horticultural awards than you can shake a stick at! Very numerous velvety flower cases become noticeable after Christmas suggesting the promise that spring is around the corner.

This Magnolia does well in all soils – including chalky ones. Small and of rounded habit, it has large, fragrant white flowers in spring that are produced in great abundance. Very attractive in both parks, hard areas and in my garden. Normally a banker for Mothering Sunday, which gets my two out of gaol!

5|10
Mature height:
5-10m

Shape of
mature tree

Flowering
trees

# MAGNOLIA x soulangeana

The most popular form of Magnolia, widely planted in parks and gardens. It has a long history, originating from Japan but was developed in France early in the 19th century. It has almost become synonymous with urban gardens in England.

Usually grown as a large shrub with a broad, round habit, the large, white, purple tinted, tulip-like flowers appear in April and May before the arrival of foliage. It tolerates heavy clay soils and is also moderately lime tolerant. Again, we buck the trend and grow this as a single stemmed tree.

5|10
Mature height:
5-10m

Shape of
mature tree

Flowering
trees

# MAGNOLIA x soulangeana Lennei

One of the very earliest clones, believed to have come from an Italian garden prior to 1850. A winner of both the First Class Certificate in 1863 and the Award of Garden Merit in 2002.

This vigorous, rounded form bears really large flowers which are rose purple on the outside and creamy white tinted with pale purple inside. A lovely choice for gardens and parks. It tolerates heavy clay soils but is only moderately lime tolerant.

Mature height: 5-10m

Shape of mature tree

Flowering trees

# MAGNOLIA Spectrum

**This Magnolia was bred in the US National Arboretum in 1963 and is a cross between Magnolia lilliflora and Magnolia sprengeri 'Diva'. It is a seedling sister of 'Galaxy'.**

A medium sized tree of conical habit formed by its ascending branches that broadens at maturity. A great choice for gardens or parks, it produces most attractive, dark purple, tulip-shaped flowers, which are lightly scented. Flowers emerge before the foliage.

It does best on moist, but free-draining, fertile soils and in sheltered or partially shaded positions.

Mature height: 10-15m

Shape of mature tree

Flowering trees

# MAGNOLIA Susan

A lovely small deciduous tree that tolerates alkaline soils. One of the so called 'Little Girl Hybrids' developed between 1955 and 1956 at the US National Arboretum, it is renowned for its profuse floral display.

Abundant deep pink-purple flowers are produced in April-June and its erect habit makes this clone a lovely addition for a small garden. We grow this variety as a tree rather than as a bush and although growth is slow the flowers never fail to disappoint.

Mature height: 3-7m

Shape of mature tree

Garden trees

Telephone 01353 720 748 • www.barcham.co.uk • Fax 01353 723 060

# MAGNOLIA Star Wars

A great name for any plant and probably sold on this basis more than any other. Introduced from Blumhardt of New Zealand and won the Award of Garden Merit in 2002 as well as the Award of Merit in 1991. The 'force' is certainly carried within this clone!

We grow this variety as a multi-stem bush. It is a campbellii x lilliflora cross and produces vigorous growth with large thick leaves after a glorious display of rich pink large goblet flowers in the spring. It is worth planting for its tremendous foliage alone.

3|7
Mature height:
3-7m

Shape of
mature tree

Garden
trees

# MALUS baccata Street Parade

This is a cultivar of the Siberian crab which is widely distributed throughout Southern Asia and was introduced into the UK in 1784.

This small crab has a tight, columnar habit and is a good choice for small gardens, street plantings or where space is limited. Plentiful, single, white flowers emerge from salmon pink buds. Shiny, purple-red fruits are produced from August onwards. Street Parade has the added advantage of being scab and mildew resistant.

| 5\|7 | | |
|---|---|---|
| Mature height: 5-7m | Shape of mature tree | Urban trees |

# MALUS Cox's Orange Pippin

**The nation's favourite eating apple, available from us as a clear stemmed full standard and grown on vigorous M16 rootstock. An ideal spring blossom specimen for any garden with the added bonus of autumn fruit.**

Profuse white flowers lead to good sized eating apples by late summer. A round headed tree that thrives on most soils, including clay, and a must for any garden orchard. Autumn colour of yellow tinged with red, is an attractive ornamental attribute.

| 5\|7 | | |
|---|---|---|
| Mature height: 5-7m | Shape of mature tree | Edible fruits |

Telephone 01353 720 748   •   www.barcham.co.uk   •   Fax 01353 723 060

# MALUS Director Moerland

A round headed variety notable for its distinctive large red / purple leaves. It was bred as a disease resistant form of Malus Profusion.

**Slightly fragrant wine red flowers are borne profusely in spring which complements emerging red leaves making this a stunning little tree for the first few growing months of the year. Best suited for gardens and parks and tolerant of most soils and conditions.**

Mature height: 5-7m | Shape of mature tree | Flowering trees

# MALUS Donald Wyman

A tried and tested performer raised by the late Donald Wyman at the Arnold Arboretum in the USA. Satisfactorily resistant to both apple scab and mildew it develops a rounded habit at maturity and is ideal for parks and gardens.

The spring flower is red to pink in bud, opening to white when in full glory. The fruit matures to a glossy vivid red and can be profuse so it is best to plant away from paved areas to avoid cleaning up. The leaves are dark green by summer.

Mature height: 5-7m | Shape of mature tree | Flowering trees

# MALUS Elstar

A cross between Golden Delicious and Ingrid Marie, this flavoursome eater is a recent addition to our range of harvest apples. Grown at Barcham as a full standard on the vigorous rootstock M16.

Pale pink flowers in the spring are an attractive aside before the fruits take shape for the autumnal bonanza. Although it prefers full sun it will tolerate semi shade but either way it tends to thrive best if the soil is free draining.

Mature height: 5-7m | Shape of mature tree | Edible fruits

# MALUS Evereste

**We recommend three crab apples in particular, one white, one red and one upright and this is one of them! A winner of the Award of Garden Merit in 2002, it was introduced in the early 1980s.**

This rounded tree of medium height has flowers that are red in bud before turning white – and the blossom is borne in profusion. The small fruits look like miniature 'Gala' and are held onto until they are taken off by birds after Christmas. On the continent they are used in displays as the little fruits hold their form so well. The orange-yellow autumn foliage also holds well. Good for gardens, parks and verges.

| 5\|7 | | |
|---|---|---|
| Mature height: 5-7m | Shape of mature tree | Flowering trees |

# MALUS floribunda

*Japanese Crab*

A most elegant crab, introduced from Japan in the early 1860s, but prone to suffer badly from Apple Scab after flowering rendering the crown to look rather threadbare from June onwards.

Very early to flower, the crimson buds open to reveal white or pale blush blossom, making this one of the most attractive crabs. The plentiful and long lasting fruits are greenish-yellow with a hint of red to them. Good for gardens, verges and parks.

| 5\|7 | | |
|---|---|---|
| Mature height: 5-7m | Shape of mature tree | Flowering trees |

Telephone 01353 720 748 ● www.barcham.co.uk ● Fax 01353 723 060

## MALUS Golden Delicious

Always derided by the purists as a tasteless French import, getting anything green and organic down my kids is a godsend in my book! Crunchy and sweet is the main criteria for my two and Golden Delicious fits the bill.

Grown at Barcham on the vigorous M16 rootstock and as a full standard, my old Writtle fruit lecturer would not be amused to hear we were growing this clone! The abundant autumnal fruit is best eaten straight off the tree as it doesn't store too well.

| Mature height: 5-7m | Shape of mature tree | Edible fruits |

## MALUS Golden Hornet

This well known garden crab has been in cultivation since the 1940s and is highly regarded for its profuse display of yellow marble sized fruits. A winner of numerous awards including the First Class Certificate in 1961.

A small tree which produces white blossom and yellow fruits, which are retained for many weeks. It has a good, oval habit and is a reliable "all-rounder", well suited to parks, verges and gardens.

| Mature height: 5-7m | Shape of mature tree | Flowering trees |

# MALUS hupehensis

A lovely crab introduced to Britain from the Far East by Ernest Wilson in 1900. Rarely planted but never forgotten if seen in full cry in the late spring.

A fine choice for gardens and parkland plantings, the ascending branches of this small tree give it a broadly columnar appearance. The fragrant flowers are pale pink while in bud, opening to white, while the small fruits are generally dark red.

| 5\|7 | | |
| :---: | :---: | :---: |
| Mature height: 5-7m | Shape of mature tree | Flowering trees |

# MALUS James Grieve

A classic addition to our eating apple range and one that is particularly popular with our despatch lads in the autumn!

Pale pink flowers in spring are followed by sweet edible fruits in late autumn to early winter. It prefers a fertile and moist free draining soil in full sun or partial shade. For best fruiting results keep the ground fallow a metre radius from the trunk and top dress this area with bark mulch. This cuts down weed competition which in turn increases fruit size.

| 5\|7 | | |
| :---: | :---: | :---: |
| Mature height: 5-7m | Shape of mature tree | Edible fruits |

● Telephone 01353 720 748 ● www.barcham.co.uk ● Fax 01353 723 060

# MALUS John Downie

**Raised in 1875, this is thought by many to be the best fruiting crab. It won the updated Award of Garden Merit from the Royal Horticultural Society in 2002.**

A small tree with an irregular, oval crown, it makes a splendid tree for gardens with limited space. The white flowers are followed by relatively large, conical orange-red fruits, which have a good flavour if required for preserves or jelly. Like all crab apples, it thrives on most soils.

Mature height: 5-7m

Shape of mature tree

Flowering trees

# MALUS Jonagold

This American apple is a cross between Jonathon and Golden Delicious. Grown on the tough M16 rootstock its white flowers in spring are attractive in their own right.

A vigorous small tree with a rounded habit, it bears an excellent crop of crisp, juicy fruits, which are full of flavour. The apples are large, greenish-yellow, lightly flushed with red, can be picked from mid October and will store well until the following spring.

Mature height: 5-7m

Shape of mature tree

Edible fruits

# MALUS Mokum

A beautiful crab for small gardens, parks and verges that is often overlooked by people favouring the more well known varieties.

The leaves of this small, oval headed tree are an eye-catching dark red and its rosy-red flowers emerge by late spring. The autumn fruits are also red giving this clone a very long season of interest. Like most crab apples, it thrives on most ground including heavier clay soils.

5|7
Mature height: 5-7m

Shape of mature tree

Flowering trees

# MALUS Pink Perfection

**A densely branched crab that is a haven for sparrows and finches always on the look out for a predator. For those of you that feed your garden birds, a twiggy and dense canopied tree is always a good place to install a nut feeder.**

The dark red buds open to reveal double, clear pink flowers, which are also fragrant. These are complemented by dense, green foliage. A great choice for parks, gardens and verges.

5|7
Mature height: 5-7m

Shape of mature tree

Flowering trees

# MALUS Profusion

A fast growing and well known crab from the late 1930s. It can occasionally get clobbered by both apple scab and mildew in the summer so it is best to avoid if replacing other Malus that may carry these pathogens.

This lovely cultivar is just about the best of those with wine red flowers. It is a small tree with a rounded crown, well suited to gardens and parks. The young, copper-crimson foliage turns bronze-green at maturity, while the rich, purple flowers, which are lightly fragrant, turn pink as the season progresses. Its fruits are small and blood red in colour.

5|7
Mature height: 5-7m

Shape of mature tree

Flowering trees

● Telephone 01353 720 748 ● www.barcham.co.uk ● Fax 01353 723 060

# MALUS Red Sentinel

Brought into cultivation in 1959, this profusely fruiting crab is a favourite for gardeners who are looking for winter interest. In some years the fruits are so numerous that the branches can weigh too heavily with them so that the crown loses its shape.

The red leaves of this small, round headed tree contrast well with its white flowers. These are followed in autumn by clusters of dark red crabs that often stay on the tree right through the winter. Good for gardens and parks.

Mature height: 5-7m | Shape of mature tree | Flowering trees

# MALUS Royalty

An upright crab, bred in Canada in the early 1950s. The foliage is so dark it is always canny not to overdo the numbers on this one. A dark foliaged tree always focuses the eye in a landscape so too many can make a garden quite dark.

Its ascending branches give Royalty a broadly columnar form. A small tree, it has shiny, rich purple foliage, which turns a vivid red in autumn. Large, purple-crimson flowers give rise to dark red fruits. Like most crabs, this is suitable for parks and gardens.

Mature height: 5-7m | Shape of mature tree | Flowering trees

# MALUS Rudolph

Another Canadian crab developed in the 1950s. I have mentioned before that we recommend one white, one pink and one upright apple, well this is the pink. The autumn colour of clear yellow is an added bonus but the main reasons we rate it so highly is its resistance to pest and disease as well as its glorious floral display.

Mature height: 5-7m

Shape of mature tree

Flowering trees

A tree of medium size, it is rather columnar when young, but the crown becomes rounded at maturity. The leaves gradually turn from copper-red to bronze-green, and rose pink flowers are followed by numerous elongated fruits, which last well. Rudolph is resistant to scab, and is particularly good as both a garden tree and for urban verge plantings.

● Telephone 01353 720 748  ● www.barcham.co.uk  ● Fax 01353 723 060

# MALUS toringo

**A delightful little dainty Japanese crab that is rarely seen but never forgotten. Its leaves are attractively lobed and it is otherwise known as Malus sieboldii, a Japanese type introduced in 1856.**

This semi-weeping, very small tree has flowers that are pink in bud, fading to white and small red or yellow fruits. Perfect for even the smallest gardens and thrives on most soils.

3|5

Mature height: 3-5m

Shape of mature tree

Flowering trees

# MALUS trilobata

A rather rare crab from the Mediterranean, so distinct it is sometimes classed as a separate genus, Eriolobus. We doggedly keep it under the Malus section and it is our recommended upright form for restricted spaces. It is a wonderfully symmetrical tree and gives a formal structure to any garden or street.

5|7

Mature height: 5-7m

Shape of mature tree

Flowering trees

A medium size tree with an upright habit, this is a good choice for parks and gardens. Its deeply lobed leaves are maple-like and take on attractive burgundy tints in autumn. It produces large, white flowers and green fruits, which are sometimes flushed red. The fruits only usually appear following hot summers.

# MESPILUS germanica

## *Medlar*

The Medlar has been in cultivation since early times, having been grown in the Emperor Charlemagne's garden. The small brown fruits it produces are only edible when "bletted" or left to turn half-rotten.

5|10
Mature height:
5-10m

Shape of
mature tree

Edible
fruits

## *Medlar*

A small, gnarled, wide spreading tree which is at home in the garden, where it produces a rounded form. It has large, hairy leaves, which turn a russet brown in autumn, and large, white flowers borne in May and June. There are some particularly interesting specimens in the Kitchen Garden at Grimsthorpe Castle in Lincolnshire that are mushroom shaped and well worth a visit in the summer.

# METASEQUOIA
## glyptostroboides
### *Dawn Redwood*

This Redwood is of great botanical interest. It was discovered in China in the 1940s, before which the genus consisted only of fossilised forms. A deciduous conifer, it has rapidly established itself as a huge urban and rural favourite. Often confused with Taxodium, it is quite different if they are seen together at close quarters.

| 20+ | | |
|---|---|---|
| Mature height: 20m+ | Shape of mature tree | Avenue trees |

Very large and statuesquely pyramidal, it makes a grand park or specimen tree, but is also good for streets and avenues with a clear stem. It has spongy, shaggy bark, and its pale green, feathery foliage turns brown in autumn. The Dawn Redwood is tolerant of air pollution, but needs a moist soil in its first year to establish successfully.

# MORUS alba Platinifolia

*White Mulberry*

**A large leaved form of the White Mulberry. I first saw this at maturity near to the coast in Brittany and its lush large foliage gives it an outstanding feeling of health and vigour.**

This is a most beautiful, small, architectural tree, perfect for parks and gardens, with a rounded habit. The white fruits, from which it takes its name, can turn pink or red – and they are both sweet and edible. The leaves of the White Mulberry are the main food of the silkworm.

Mature height: 5-10m | Shape of mature tree | Edible fruits

# Morus nigra

*Black Mulberry*

Brought to Britain by the Romans and widely planted by James I, who wished to establish a silk industry – only to find that silkworms feed exclusively on the White Mulberry!

A medium tree of great dignity and beauty, it has a gnarled, rugged trunk and most attractive, heart shaped leaves. The deep purple fruits, which look like large loganberries are tasty and have a variety of culinary uses.

It has a domed, rounded habit, giving it a most architectural appeal. Very long-lived, but not as slow growing as is often supposed.

Mature height: 5-10m | Shape of mature tree | Edible fruits

# NOTHOFAGUS antarctica

*Antarctic Beech*

A native of Chile and introduced to Britain in the early 1830s, this beech is a fast grower. Many see this in leaf and take it for an evergreen tree but it is deciduous. Its bark is dark and covered with attractive white lenticels.

Of rounded habit and medium to large size, this has small, heart shaped leaves which turn yellow as the year progresses. Very good for parks and public spaces, it does best in a sunny position and fairly fertile soil. It will not tolerate planting in calcareous soils.

| 15\|20 | | |
|---|---|---|
| Mature height: 15-20m | Shape of mature tree | Parkland trees |

# NOTHOFAGUS dombeyi

Native of both Argentina and Chile and introduced into the UK in 1916, this wonderful evergreen tree is rarely seen. The only mature specimen I have come across is at Calderstone Park, Liverpool, and is the delight of the resident arborist there.

Dark, shiny leaves may sometimes be lost in cold winters but the tree is hardy enough to come back in the spring / summer. It is both wide spreading and very striking, especially in the winter. There is always a waiting list for this tree as we grow so few of them, so get in early to avoid disappointment!

| 10\|15 | | |
|---|---|---|
| Mature height: 10-15m | Shape of mature tree | Garden trees |

# NYSSA sylvatica

Introduced from America in 1750, this is widely regarded as the most attractive of all the native trees from the States. It won the Award of Garden Merit in 2002.

Pyramidal when young it can resemble Quercus palustris in shape and habit, and certainly rivals it for autumn colour when its foliage turns magnificent reds, oranges and yellows. The dark glossy green leaves are narrowly oval and can reach 15cm in length. They do not tolerate lime soils so please bear this in mind if you choose one.

| 15\|20 | | |
|---|---|---|
| Mature height: 15-20m | Shape of mature tree | Autumn colour |

● Telephone 01353 720 748  ● www.barcham.co.uk  ● Fax 01353 723 060

# OLEA europaea
*Olive*

**Surely the quintessential tree of the Mediterranean and cultivated virtually since the beginning of time, the Olive is only really hardy in the milder areas of Britain. I have one thriving in my garden in Rutland but I have yet to reap a harvest. However, it is worth growing for its evergreen foliage alone.**

A small tree with a rounded form, it can take on an attractively gnarled appearance as it develops. It has small, leathery grey-green leaves and small, white, fragrant flowers. We grow olive as both half standard and full standard and they can benefit greatly by a severe biannual prune in April.

5|7
Mature height: 5-7m

Shape of mature tree

Edible fruits

# OSTRYA carpinifolia
## *Hop Hornbeam*

The Hop Hornbeam is so-called because it looks like a Hornbeam and its creamy white flowers resemble hops. Introduced in 1724 from Southern Europe and Western Asia it won the Award of Merit in the hot summer of 1976.

**This medium to large tree is good for parkland settings, verges and many urban locations. It looks particularly good in spring with its display of yellow-green catkins. A really tough tree, which will tolerate most conditions.**

15|20

Mature height: 15-20m

Shape of mature tree

Clay soils

● Telephone 01353 720 748 ● www.barcham.co.uk ● Fax 01353 723 060

# PARROTIA persica

*Persian Ironwood*

Persian Ironwood is usually grown as a large shrub, and was formerly classified as a species of Hamamelis. It takes its name from the well known German horticulturalist, FW Parrot and is a native of Iran. There are some particularly nice specimens at the Westonbirt Arboretum near Stroud.

5|10
Mature height: 5-10m

Shape of mature tree

Autumn colour

A beautiful, small, rounded tree with grey-brown bark which becomes attractively mottled with yellow. This really is one of the finest small trees for autumn colour, giving a display of crimson, purple, red and gold. A splendid choice for gardens and parks, it does well on most soils, including chalk.

# PARROTIA persica Vanessa

Vanessa has a more tree-like form than the species, and was selected as a seedling in the Netherlands in the mid 1970s. A great favourite at Barcham, it produces small but vivid red flowers at maturity.

A small tree with a broad, oval crown. Vanessa gives a stunning display of autumn colour and is ideal for specimen planting in a park or large garden. Prior to that, it displays red shoots and bronze edges to its deep green leaves. It does well on most soils and will tolerate chalk.

5|10
Mature height: 5-10m

Shape of mature tree

Autumn Colour

# PAULOWNIA tomentosa

## *Foxglove Tree*

**One of the most spectacular of ornamental flowering trees, the Foxglove Tree takes its name from the foxglove-like flowers, which are formed in autumn, but do not open until the following spring. Introduced from China in 1834, its wood is much prized in Japan for furniture making.**

Amazingly, a mature tree in its native environment can produce up to 20 million seeds per year which converts to over 85,000 seeds per ounce. The tree was named after Anna Pavlovna, daughter of Czar Paul 1 and wife of Prince Willem of the Netherlands. It is so quick to grow in its younger years that its growth rings have been recorded at three every inch. However, our more temperate climate slows it down and any growth under pencil thickness generally succumbs to winter frosts which contribute to its overall broadness. The flower cases are formed in the autumn so if the temperature dips below 5 degrees Celsius for too long, no flower will develop the following spring.

A fast growing, medium to large, round headed tree. It does best in a sunny, reasonably sheltered site, where it will produce a breathtaking display of violet-blue and yellow flowers in May once it is established. Its large, hairy leaves can reach 30cm or more across.

**10|15**
Mature height: 10-15m

Shape of mature tree

Flowering trees

# PHELLODENDRON amurense

## *Amur Cork Tree*

**A small genus from East Asia, resembling Ailanthus that was introduced into the UK in 1885. It is more suited to rural rather than urban settings but is rarely seen in Britain.**

Large leaves, over 25cm in length, and silver, hairy winter buds distinguish this tree from others but it is the corky bark of mature trees that is its most impressive feature. An unusual tree for arboricultural collectors.

Mature height: 10-15m | Shape of mature tree | Parkland trees

# PHOTINIA x fraseri Red Robin

This beautiful clone was bred in New Zealand and won the Award of Garden Merit in 2002. Much is made of its foliage but more mature plants give a profuse display of white flower in the spring that contrasts magnificently with emerging red leaves.

This small, evergreen tree is often grown as a shrub. As a tree, it develops a rounded crown; its new leaves open to red before hardening to green as they age. Frequent pruning encourages glorious red foliage and makes it every bit as beautiful as Pieris formosa. Lovely in gardens and parks. It is mostly grown as a shrub but we grow it as a standard tree, mainly for stilted screening.

Mature height: 5-7m | Shape of mature tree | Privacy raised screening

● Telephone 01353 720 748  ● www.barcham.co.uk  ● Fax 01353 723 060

# PHYLLOSTACHYS aurea

## *Golden Bamboo*

In the Far East the canes of this Bamboo are used for walking sticks and umbrella handles, while in America they are turned into fishing rods. Introduced from China in the 1870s it won the Award of Garden Merit in 2002.

This Bamboo forms clumps of canes which are bright green at first and then mature to a pale creamy yellow. The young shoots, which it produces in spring, are edible but beware, this plant is not for the faint hearted as it is extremely vigorous!

Mature height: 3-5m    Shape of mature tree    Evergreen trees

# PHYLLOSTACHYS nigra

## *Black Bamboo*

**Black Bamboo is surely the most dramatic of all. It is less vigorous than the golden equivalent but that didn't stop me reducing mine to 5cm off ground level in March 2009 to stimulate a fresh display.**

This stylish Bamboo has a gracefully arching habit and does best in a sunny position. The canes begin as green before becoming mottled with brown and then black. The shoots which it produces in spring are edible.

Mature height: 3-5m    Shape of mature tree    Evergreen trees

# PICEA omorika

## *Serbian Spruce*

The Serbian Spruce was widely distributed through much of Europe before the onset of the Ice Age. It was not, however, introduced to Britain until the late 1880s. Similar in looks to a traditional Christmas tree when young, its branches adopt a graceful pendulous habit when mature.

Certainly one of the most beautiful of Spruces, this is a medium to large, slender columnar tree which grows quickly. It tolerates air pollution, calcareous soils and is good as an evergreen street or avenue subject. If planting in a public area my advice is to install after Christmas and not before!

Mature height: 15-20m    Shape of mature tree    Evergreen trees

# PICEA pungens Hoopsii

This form of Colorado blue spruce is slow growing but highly ornamental. Introduced in the mid 1950s it won the Award of Garden Merit in 2002 and like most conifers it prefers free draining soils.

Vividly glaucous blue leaves and dense conical habit make this small tree a real contrast in a garden or parkland setting. It is so slow to grow that it is perceived as expensive for its size supplied but it offers a unique colour to a garden.

Mature height: 5-10m    Shape of mature tree    Evergreen trees

# PINUS nigra Austriaca

*Austrian Pine*

Sometimes referred to as 'Black Pine' or 'Pinus nigra nigra' this tough two needled evergreen was introduced in the mid 1830s. Its needles are much greener and longer than Scots Pine and its growth more solid giving it a denser habit than our native pine. Stand behind a maturing Austrian Pine on a windy day and be amazed how the wind is diffused by the needles to calm the air flow.

A first rate choice for coastal areas and exposed, windswept sites, it thrives even in very chalky soils. This large evergreen has a pyramidal form, but retains its bushy, juvenile appearance much longer than Scots Pine. It is from ancient genera, so its toughness is based on a very solid track record.

Mature height: 20m+    Shape of mature tree    Evergreen trees

# PINUS mugo Mops

## *Swiss Mountain Pine, Mugo Pine*

**Introduced in the early 1950s, this clone of the dwarf shrub pine is considered by many to be the finest. Pinus mugo can be very variable in size and habit with recorded mature heights of between 1 metre and 15 metres but 'Mops' rarely gets larger than 1.5 metres.**

This is a new addition to our range and should be online in containers by September 2012. It is a very versatile garden or landscape plant, mimicking a bonsai effect of traditional pine and requiring minimal maintenance. It is tough and is suited to most soil types including shallow chalk.

Mature height:
1-2m

Shape of
mature tree

Evergreen
trees

# PINUS pinaster

## *Bournemouth Pine, Maritime Pine*

A highly useful introduction from the Western Mediterranean. Introduced in the 16th century it thrives on light sandy soils and tolerates coastal conditions. It won the Award of Garden Merit in 2002. Commonly planted on England's South coast from which it derives its common name.

Sparsely branched, it can get quite large and develops a dark reddish brown patchwork bark at maturity. Shiny brown cones are produced about 18cm long which compliment the long leaves that are grown in pairs. It is very important in Western France where it supplies industry with large quantities of turpentine and resin.

Mature height:
15-20m

Shape of
mature tree

Evergreen
trees

# PINUS pinea

## *Italian Stone Pine*

The Stone Pine is sometimes also known as the Umbrella Pine. Its seeds, which when roasted, are an essential ingredient of the well known Italian pesto sauce. Unlike other Pines we grow, this one is produced as a half standard or standard tree with a well developed rounded crown.

A distinct and rather picturesque medium tree, this Pine does well in coastal locations and on light, sandy soils. Its bark is gorgeously craggy, flaking off easily when disturbed. A native of the Mediterranean, it won the Award of Garden Merit in 2002.

Mature height:
10-15m

Shape of
mature tree

Evergreen
trees

**Barcham**

P

# PINUS radiata
## *Monterey Pine*

This makes a large tree with a deeply fissured bark and a dense crown of branches supporting needles in threes up to 15cm in length. Introduced in 1833 by David Douglas from California, it won the Award of Garden Merit in 2002.

**Cones are borne in whorls along the branches and often remain intact for several years. A very useful subject for coastal areas as it is quick to grow and able to withstand strong salt laden winds.**

| 20+ | | |
|---|---|---|
| Mature height: 20m+ | Shape of mature tree | Evergreen trees |

# PINUS sylvestris
## *Scots Pine*

The Scots Pine is the only Pine native to Britain. A familiar sight in bleak and inhospitable landscapes, it can be grown as a tall stemmed or a low, spreading subject. Its paired needles can be very variable in colour from green to almost blue, especially when juvenile. It is very quick to develop a symbiotic relationship with mycorrhiza which helps sustain vigorous growth.

| 20+ | | |
|---|---|---|
| Mature height: 20m+ | Shape of mature tree | Evergreen trees |

This large evergreen tree is distinctive by its tall, bare trunk and broadly pyramidal crown. It is best suited in parks, gardens, heath land and woodlands. It is tolerant of most soils but never reaches its true potential in areas prone to flooding. As a cautionary note, it is worth sticking with Austrian Pine for coastal conditions as Scots Pine rarely seems to thrive near the coast.

# PINUS sylvestris Fastigiata

## *Sentinel Pine*

A wonderfully columnar form of Scots Pine, so tight in habit that one has to get quite close to indentify it. There are some nicely maturing specimens in the conifer garden at the Harlow Carr arboretum. The needles appear almost blue when young giving it a highly ornamental feel.

Introduced circa 1856, it is naturally occurring in Europe. It can reach over 10 metres tall if it isn't hampered by snow and ice build up which can cause it to fracture. However, there are no such problems in the UK making this a fabulous choice for many aspects.

Mature height: 5-10m | Shape of mature tree | Narrow trees

# PINUS wallichiana

## *Bhutan Pine*

A native of the Himalayas, this wonderfully attractive soft needled pine was introduced to Britain in the early 1820s and is also known by many as Pinus griffithii. A winner of the Award of Garden Merit in 2002 and the Award of Merit in 1979, it is a worthy subject for any large garden.

Elegant and most ornamental, this large, rather conical tree has blue-green foliage and pendent cones which become covered in resin. It is moderately lime tolerant but shallow chalk soils should be avoided. It offers a unique softness to a large garden and so easily draws the eye.

Mature height: 20m+ | Shape of mature tree | Evergreen trees

# PLATANUS x hispanica (acerifolia)
## *London Plane*

First recorded in the early 1660s, the London Plane was extensively planted as a street tree in the capital due to its tolerance of air pollution and of pruning. It is believed that it was significantly responsible for clearing up the smog laden air resulting from the industrial revolution.

A large, fast growing tree with a broadly oval crown. One of its main features is the trunk, which flakes to reveal a patchwork of green, white and cream. The leaves are large, deeply lobed and palmate. The rounded fruit clusters, produced in strings, resemble little baubles, which hang from the branches for much of the year. Still a good choice for urban plantings, it is also great for parkland.

20+

Mature height:
20m+

Shape of
mature tree

Urban
trees

## *London Plane*

Reputedly the oldest Plane tree in England is in the Bishops Palace Garden at Ely. Planted by Bishop Gunning more than 300 years ago it is one of the most impressive trees in Britain, and just a stones throw from Barcham.

● Telephone 01353 720 748  ● www.barcham.co.uk  ● Fax 01353 723 060

# PLATANUS x hispanica
# Alphens Globe

A dwarfing clone top worked onto a Platanus x hispanica stem ideal for restricted urban areas. More popular as a choice of street tree in continental Europe, this style of tree has never really caught on in the UK but it does have its uses.

This has a similar effect and usage to Fraxinus ornus Meczek and Acer campestre Nanum. Good for areas where size is restrictive, this clone produces a ball of dwarfing foliage requiring little maintenance.

Mature height: 5-10m

Shape of mature tree

Urban trees

# PLATANUS orientalis Digitata

**One of the most striking of Planes, it is also known as the Chennar Tree, and often provides shaded meeting places in southern European villages. There is a wonderful example of its parent, Platanus orientalis, in the Bishops Palace garden in Ely not too far from Barcham.**

This has similar, attractively flaking bark to the London Plane, but has deeply cut five lobed leaves. A large tree with a generally rounded habit, it can attain a very great age. Magnificent in parkland and large estates as well as gracing the main arterial roads of central London.

Mature height: 20m+

Shape of mature tree

Urban trees

# PLATANUS orientalis
# Minaret

Similar to 'Digitata' this clone was planted along the pavement avenues of O'Connell Street in Dublin to great effect. Very neat in habit when young, it develops a broad crown much the same as its parent, Platanus orientalis, when maturing.

Lovely cut leaves and a good pyramidal habit makes this a good choice for urban streets and parkland. Reputed to have good resistance to anthracnose, but I have not seen it for long enough to make judgement.

Mature height: 20m+

Shape of mature tree

Urban trees

# PODOCARPUS macrophyllus

*Kusamaki*

**This highly distinctive species is a native of Japan and China, introduced in the 1860s. It is probably the hardiest of the varieties available, tolerating down to -20 degrees Celsius.**

The 10-15cm leaves, bright green above and slightly glaucous beneath, are arranged in dense spirals on the stem. A conifer in the gymnosperm group that bears naked seed referred to as fruit. It is best to stay clear of heavy clay with poor drainage as well as chalky soils.

| Mature height: 3-5m | Shape of mature tree | Garden trees |

# POPULUS alba

*White Poplar*

The fast growing White Poplar is ideal for exposed and coastal plantings. Long naturalised in the UK, it was first introduced from South Eastern Europe. Its vivid foliage is most spectacular on a bright sunny day against a cloudless sky.

Ultimately a large tree of fairly rounded form, it has green leaves, the undersides of which are silver-white, turning yellow in autumn. It is a tough tree, but it needs to be given plenty of space for its extensive root system to develop. A good choice for calcareous soils.

| Mature height: 20m+ | Shape of mature tree | Coastal sites |

# POPULUS alba Raket

This cultivar of White Poplar was raised in Holland in the 1950s for urban use. It is a particularly useful choice for coastal settings where the sea breezes constantly flicker the silver white leaves to provide splendid contrast.

It is notable for its columnar and slender habit when young but it still makes a formidable tree when mature so care should be taken to give it enough space to colonise. It thrives on most soils and is quick to grow.

| Mature height: 20m+ | Shape of mature tree | Coastal sites |

Telephone 01353 720 748 • www.barcham.co.uk • Fax 01353 723 060

# POPULUS x candicans Aurora

**Given the Award of Merit in 1954, this highly showy tree is both vigorous and instantly recognisable.**

The leaves are randomly variegated, especially when young, with coloured creamy white leaves that are also often tinged pink. Older leaves turn green and mysteriously newly transplanted trees show no sign of variegation either until they settle down in the second year. For best results, hard prune the shoots in winter and you will be rewarded by a magnificent display the following growing season.

15|20 — Mature height: 15-20m | Shape of mature tree | Variegated trees

# POPULUS nigra
*Black Poplar*

The Black Poplar, a native of Europe and Western Asia, is rarely found these days. We are involved with a project to propagate native Black Poplar from both male and female trees in Essex so we will soon have these marketable.

Cultivated for a long time and prized for its timber, this makes a large, rounded and heavy-branched tree, characterised by its burred trunk and glabrous twigs. Very good for parks and woodland.

20+ — Mature height: 20m+ | Shape of mature tree | Native trees

# POPULUS nigra Italica
## *Lombardy Poplar*

The Lombardy poplar is a male clone, propagated from cuttings taken in Lombardy in the 1700s. It is a particularly tough tree even coping with coastal exposure. Introduced to the UK in 1758 it won the Award of Garden Merit in 2002.

These are the trees that line mile after mile (or should that be kilometre after kilometre?) of French roads. Very tall, tightly columnar and of uniform habit, they make a fine windbreak or screen, and are also good for specimen planting in parks. One of the very best for verges and avenues.

Mature height: 20m+ | Shape of mature tree | Narrow trees

# POPULUS serotina Aurea
## *Golden Poplar*

**Derived from a sport taken at Van Geert's nursery in Ghent in 1871, this won the Award of Garden Merit in 2002.**

Large and fast growing, this tree is also known as Populus x canadensis serotina Aurea. It sometimes produces a rather uneven crown so it is best for parkland. Its leaves, coppery red when young, are late to show and its catkins have conspicuous red anthers. Like all Poplars, it thrives on most soils.

Mature height: 15-20m | Shape of mature tree | Parkland trees

● Telephone 01353 720 748 ● www.barcham.co.uk ● Fax 01353 723 060

# POPULUS tremula
## *Aspen*

The shimmering of Aspen leaves, set in motion on even the most gentle of breezes, provides a wonderful rustling sound in the landscape reminiscent of slow cascading water.

**Grey catkins appear in early spring, while the serrated leaves turn clear yellow in autumn and often remain on the tree for many weeks. The Aspen is a medium to large tree with a rounded habit. Well suited to verges and parkland.**

Mature height: 15-20m

Shape of mature tree

Parkland trees

# POPULUS tremula Erecta

Widely used as a street tree in the USA this underused tree was first discovered in a Swedish woodland and still bears the name 'Swedish Upright'. Similar in shape and habit to the Lombardy poplar it offers far more ornamental interest with bronze foliage emerging in April once the long catkins have finished.

We rate this highly as a tightly columnar tree that is very suitable for planting within an urban environment. The trembling leaves turn a lovely orange yellow in the autumn and this clone requires very little maintenance. If you visit Barcham you will notice a short avenue of these adjacent to our roadside field.

As I am writing this I am looking at one I planted three years ago in my garden. It is just beginning its second summer flush of reddish foliage and its rustle somehow calms the space around it.

Mature height: 15-20m

Shape of mature tree

Narrow trees

# PRUNUS Accolade

This Flowering Cherry is a cross between Prunus sargentii and Prunus x subhirtella and so inherits the best features of both, namely profuse pink flowers in spring as well as a smattering in the winter. This great clone is well proven, winning the First Class Certificate in 1954, the Award of Merit in 1952 and the updated Award of Garden Merit in 2002.

An outstandingly fine small tree with a rounded and spreading habit, its semi-double pink blossoms are hard to rival. Tolerant of most soils, including calcareous ones, this is a good choice for streets, parks and gardens.

Mature height: 5-10m

Shape of mature tree

Flowering trees

● Telephone 01353 720 748 ● www.barcham.co.uk ● Fax 01353 723 060

# PRUNUS Amanogawa

This late April and early May blossoming Japanese Cherry is also known as Prunus serrulata Erecta Miyoshi. A well used and recognised variety, it won the Award of Garden Merit in 2002.

Perfect as a street tree or garden tree where space is at a premium, this tightly columnar cultivar is often grown as a feathered tree to maximise the number of semi-double, shell pink flowers it produces. The young leaves are a copper-bronze. Tolerant of most free draining soils.

Mature height: 5-10m | Shape of mature tree | Flowering trees

# PRUNUS avium

*Wild Cherry*

The red-brown wood of the Wild Cherry is used in cabinet making and for musical instruments and pipes. Although its own fruits tend to be bitter, it is one of the parents of most European cultivated Cherries.

It thrives on most free draining soils and prefers to be planted in a woodland or parkland setting.

Mature height: 10-15m | Shape of mature tree | Native trees

One of the most attractive of our native, woodland trees, this becomes a medium to large tree with a broadly rounded form. Its white flowers in spring are followed by foliage which often shows good autumn colouring of red and gold. A good tree for parks and woodlands.

# PRUNUS avium Plena

**This wonderful double flowering version of our native Wild Cherry has been in cultivation since the early 1700s and is still a favourite today. Its mass of double white flowers are absolutely superb when in full swing.**

Although it is best suited to parkland / woodland planting it is also a very useful urban tree, coping well with reflected heat and light bouncing back from hard surfaces. It often retains a strong apically dominant leader making the trunk easy to crown lift over time. Given the right conditions the autumn foliage can also be glorious, and like most cherries it thrives on free draining soils.

Mature height: 10-15m

Shape of mature tree

Urban trees

# PRUNUS cerasifera Nigra

*Purple Leaved Plum*

Introduced in the early 1900s this form of the Cherry Plum (or Myrobolan) usually sets only a few red fruits. A popular tree, often planted in city streets or verges, it is easy to maintain in a garden as it reacts well to very severe pruning.

A small tree with a rounded form, it is most notable for its purple leaves and stems. Early pink spring flowers fade to white before the leaves take full effect. This is a robust performer, thriving on most free draining soils.

Mature height: 5-10m

Shape of mature tree

Red/purple foliage

● Telephone 01353 720 748  ● www.barcham.co.uk  ● Fax 01353 723 060

# PRUNUS Cheals Weeping

This well known garden tree has been oversold by garden centres for years but still represents one of the best weeping cherry cultivars in production. It requires very little maintenance, thrives in most free draining soils and never fails to perform.

Rather similar to Prunus Kiku-shidare Sakura, this has a more steeply weeping habit. It is a small tree, and is stunning in spring when it bears double pink flowers. An excellent choice for gardens where space is limited.

Mature height: 3-5m | Shape of mature tree | Garden trees

# PRUNUS domestica Victoria

The nation's favourite eating plum, grown on a colt root stock here at Barcham as a full standard. The small white flowers that emerge in the spring are superseded by good sized red blushed fruits that beckon to us, birds and insects alike.

Our despatch teams tend to gorge themselves with the plums prior to autumn delivery so don't be surprised to take delivery of baron plants! Nutritious free draining soils free from grass competition within a metre radius from the trunk provide best results for your fruiting harvest.

Mature height: 5-10m | Shape of mature tree | Edible fruits

# PRUNUS dulcis

### *Common Almond*

I was shown a lovely painting of Hampstead Garden Suburb depicting a Victorian tree-lined avenue of Almonds in full flower which prompted me to bring back this old favourite into our range. However it is fraught with difficulty as they tend to attract every insect pest and fungal mildew under the sun so beware!!

Its pink, single and double flowers can reach up to 5cm across before the foliage emerges to create a lovely effect. It is always best to plant on free draining soils where no other Prunus have been, to try and avoid pest and disease build up.

Mature height: 5-10m | Shape of mature tree | Edible nuts

# PRUNUS fruiticosa Globosa

This man-made tree has its uses in urban environments where space is limited. Small white flowers in spring are replaced by a dense canopy of small vivid green leaves that turn a glorious orange / red in the autumn.

A top worked, dwarfing clone which forms a compact and rounded crown. Budded onto Colt rootstock, Prunus avium is used as the inter-stock, with fruiticosa Globosa top grafted to form the crown. The avium inter-stock gives the height, while the Colt rootstock prevents pavement heave. It requires virtually no maintenance, and is an admirable urban tree.

| 5\|7 | | |
|---|---|---|
| Mature height: 5-7m | Shape of mature tree | Urban trees |

# PRUNUS x gondouinii Schnee

A most attractive form of Duke Cherry with lustrous and large green leaves that give a good autumnal display of gold and orange. It is a cross between Prunus avium and Prunus cerasus and although not commonly planted it has considerable merit.

This small, rounded tree is perfect for gardens, parks and street plantings. The large, white, single flowers are borne in late April and early May. It thrives best in free draining soils and there is a historic avenue of them in Battersea Park, London.

| 5\|10 | | |
|---|---|---|
| Mature height: 5-10m | Shape of mature tree | Garden trees |

# PRUNUS x hillieri Spire

**A cross between Prunus sargentii and Prunus yedoensis raised in the late 1920s. The original tree now stands at 10 metres high and its autumn colour can be a joy to behold. It has had many accolades over the years and won the Award of Garden Merit in 2002.**

This ranks as one of the finest of small street trees, and it is also excellent in gardens and parks. With its tight, upright habit and profusion of pink flowers, it is ideal for most sites where space is limited. Rather slow growing.

| 5\|10 | | |
|---|---|---|
| Mature height: 5-10m | Shape of mature tree | Narrow trees |

Telephone 01353 720 748 • www.barcham.co.uk • Fax 01353 723 060

# PRUNUS incisa Louisa Leo

A superb small tree for street and urban plantings. Often referred to as the Fuji Cherry, its dainty small leaves turn wonderfully in the autumn to orange and red. It does not benefit from being planted in waterlogged soils.

**This is a small to medium sized tree with a narrow, columnar habit, and its pink-white single flowers are freely produced in April, along with the foliage. It is fairly similar to Prunus Okame as they share the same parentage.**

Mature height: 5-10m | Shape of mature tree | Flowering trees

# PRUNUS Kanzan

A very widely planted and most popular Flowering Cherry. Introduced in the early 1900s, it has won numerous awards culminating in the Award of Garden Merit in 2002. Its large green leaves can turn to a glorious display in the autumn but first emerge a coppery red.

It is more vigorous but otherwise similar to Pink Perfection.

Mature height: 5-10m | Shape of mature tree | Flowering trees

This cherry has stiffly ascending branches forming a columnar crown when young before becoming more rounded at maturity. It is of medium height and reliably produces plenty of very showy, dark pink flowers in the spring. Sometimes rather too vigorous for paved areas, it is, nevertheless, good in parks.

# PRUNUS laurocerasus Angustifolia

Introduced in the early 1800s we grow this laurel as a semi-mature tree with a clear stem of 1.8-2m, ideal for stilted screening.

There are few evergreen trees tolerant of being in shadow, but this cultivar will thrive in either sun or shade. It has ascending branches and small leaves resembling those of Prunus lusitanica or Zabeliana. It produces white flowers in the spring and reacts well to pruning if required.

Mature height: 5-7m

Shape of mature tree

Privacy raised screening

# PRUNUS laurocerasus Latifolia

**A tree form of laurel, grown as a standard. White flowers in the spring and year round evergreen leaves marks this clone as very useful for those requiring privacy.**

Hedging laurel often takes as much horizontal space as vertical space in a garden, and with small areas this can be problematic. This clone of laurel has thinner leaves than that of Prunus Rotundifolia and also runs up as a standard plant so the screening is effective beyond the fence line without encroaching into valuable garden space at ground level.

Mature height: 5-7m

Shape of mature tree

Privacy raised screening

# PRUNUS laurocerasus Rotundifolia

*Laurel*

Cherry laurel was introduced from its native Eastern Europe in 1576 and is now naturalised over much of the UK. It relies on the trace element magnesium so if your hedge is yellowing you now know what to apply! It does not thrive on shallow chalky soils.

A particularly bushy, rounded form, this cultivar is ideal for hedging and screening. It is a very versatile plant as it can be savagely pruned back to bare wood and still only take a few months to regain its screening use.

Mature height: 5m

Shape of mature tree

Hedging trees

● Telephone 01353 720 748  ●  www.barcham.co.uk  ●  Fax 01353 723 060

# PRUNUS lusitanica

*Portugal Laurel*

Portugal Laurel is widely used for hedging, but also makes a fine, specimen tree if required. It is prettier than common laurel with red stems and narrower leaves but it is just as durable. White flowers in the spring are an added bonus.

**We offer them as half-standards. Grown as a tree, it remains small and has a good rounded habit, and it does well on most soils, including shallow chalk. Very attractive as a hedge, giving year-round interest and cover to many small birds. Ideal for gardens and parks.**

5|10
Mature height: 5-10m | Shape of mature tree | Hedging trees

# PRUNUS maackii Amber Beauty

A Dutch selection of the Manchurian Cherry. Thriving on most free draining soils the white flowers in spring are more akin to Bird Cherry than anything else and their effect is lovely against a clear blue sky.

Stunning in winter with its smoothly polished, golden stems, this cultivar of medium height and rounded form is early into leaf in spring. It is a stout and vigorous grower tolerating the harsher aspects of our urban environments.

I have seen this clone planted as a street tree in Portsmouth and it makes a fantastically stocky tree with a rounded crown as it drifts into maturity.

5|10
Mature height: 5-10m | Shape of mature tree | Bark interest

## PRUNUS Okame

This very pretty cherry is derived from Prunus incisa and was raised by Captain Collingwood Ingram in the 1940s. A winner of the Award of Garden Merit in 2002, its dainty foliage produces a great autumnal display of orange and reds.

A narrow, columnar, small tree, Okame produces a mass of profuse rich pink flowers in late March and early April. It is a splendid choice for gardens and parks. Like most of its type it is not suited to waterlogged soils.

| 5\|7 | Shape of mature tree | Garden trees |
|---|---|---|
| Mature height: 5-7m | | |

## PRUNUS padus

### *Bird Cherry*

The Bird Cherry, a native of Britain as well as the rest of Europe, is a relatively late flowerer. It is a tough tree, withstanding the rigours of the urban environment but like other cherries does not thrive on waterlogged ground.

The white flowers of the Bird Cherry are produced in May in hanging racemes. The black fruits in late summer are edible but rather bitter. Luscious and large green leaves turn yellow to bronze in autumn. This is a rounded tree of medium height, and is good in parks, gardens and woodlands.

| 10\|15 | Shape of mature tree | Native trees |
|---|---|---|
| Mature height: 10-15m | | |

Telephone 01353 720 748  •  www.barcham.co.uk  •  Fax 01353 723 060

# PRUNUS padus Albertii

This clone of Bird Cherry has been cultivated since the 1900s and is probably the best clone for urban plantings where space is more restricted. The crown is very ascending when young before developing into an oval to rounded shape at maturity.

A rather good choice for garden, street and verge planting, this very free flowering form has an excellent track record for requiring little maintenance. It thrives on most soils but is best suited to free draining sites.

Mature height: 10-15m

Shape of mature tree

Urban trees

# PRUNUS padus Watereri

Sometimes referred to as Prunus padus Grandiflora, this clone of Bird Cherry was introduced slightly after 'Albertii' in the early 1900s. It won the Award of Garden Merit in 2002 and is a popular choice for amenity planting.

Remarkable for its long white racemes – up to 20cm long – this cultivar is of medium height and with a rounded, rather spreading habit. A good selection for parks and other open spaces but is too vigorous for streets. Quick to grow in the first few years it tolerates most soils.

Mature height: 10-15m

Shape of mature tree

Parkland trees

# PRUNUS Pandora

This wonderful Prunus yedoensis cross is a great choice for an urban garden or street. It won the Award of Merit in 1939 and the updated Award of Garden Merit in 2002. It has relatively small leaves for a cherry and requires very little maintenance for so much ornamental interest.

Pandora makes only a small tree, but its ascending branches, which give its broadly columnar habit, become smothered by pale pink blossom in March and early April. The bronze-red leaves in autumn also provide a wonderful show. It thrives best on free draining sites.

5|10
Mature height: 5-10m

Shape of mature tree

Flowering trees

● Telephone 01353 720 748 ● www.barcham.co.uk ● Fax 01353 723 060

# PRUNUS pennsylvanica Auburn Splendour

**The species from which this clone was created was introduced into the UK from North America in 1773. It has the prettiness of Tibetan cherry but the lustiness of Prunus avium Plena. It is not suited to waterlogged ground.**

Although the bark on this clone is not quite as striking as that of Prunus serrula Tibetica it is a fairly close run thing. Round headed and tough, it is an excellent choice for verge, parkland and garden planting where all year round interest is preferred. Its flowers are white but of no great consequence compared to its reflective bark.

| 10\|15 | | |
| Mature height: 10-15m | Shape of mature tree | Bark interest |

# PRUNUS Pink Perfection

A British-bred form of flowering cherry that started its commercial origins in about 1935 and won the Award of Garden Merit in 2002. It prefers free draining soils and will generally suffer if waterlogged.

Similar in some ways to Kanzan, which we believe to be one of its parents, Pink Perfection is less vigorous. Its double flowers, dark pink in bud, opening slightly paler, are borne in long clusters. It has a broadly oval crown and is of medium to large form. Suitable for verges, broad streets and parks.

| 5\|10 | | |
| Mature height: 5-10m | Shape of mature tree | Flowering trees |

# PRUNUS Royal Burgundy

This Flowering Cherry is rather like a purple-leaved equivalent of the well known Prunus Kanzan. Fairly new to our range, it gives wonderful contrast to a garden with its spectacular foliage and flower display. Historically Prunus cerasifera Nigra is thought of as the choice for purple leaf interest but this clone provides real competition.

5|10

Mature height:
5-10m

Shape of
mature tree

Red/purple
foliage

A small tree with ascending branches, it forms an oval to rounded crown at maturity. Its double, shell pink flowers are set against beautiful, wine-red foliage to create an eye-catching effect. Lovely in parks and gardens but like most cherries it prefers a free draining soil.

Telephone 01353 720 748   •   www.barcham.co.uk   •   Fax 01353 723 060

# PRUNUS sargentii

Introduced from its native Japan in 1890 this is widely regarded as one of the loveliest of flowering cherries – and with the advantage of its blossom usually being ignored by bullfinches. A winner of numerous accolades culminating in the Award of Garden Merit in 2002.

A superb, small tree of rounded habit, and a great choice for gardens, parks and streets.  It bears abundant, single, pink flowers in March and April, and is one of the first to take on its autumn tints of orange and crimson, which complement its chestnut-brown bark so effectively.

Mature height: 5-10m | Shape of mature tree | Flowering trees

# PRUNUS sargentii Rancho

**Sometimes too close to call from straight forward Prunus sargentii, this flowering cherry was raised in the USA in the 1950s and came across to be grown by European nurseries shortly afterwards.**

A broadly columnar form of the species, it is of similarly low height, and is just the job where space is rather restricted.  It bears abundant, single, pink flowers in March and April, and is one of the first to take on its autumn tints of orange and crimson. Its bark is noticeably darker than most cherries and it thrives best on free draining soils.

Mature height: 5-10m | Shape of mature tree | Flowering trees

# PRUNUS x schmittii

This Prunus avium cross originates back to 1923 and can grow more than 15 metres given suitable conditions. Sometimes too vigorous for streets, it is better placed on green verges or gardens where it needs little or no maintenance.

It is most remarkable for its polished, red-brown bark that improves with every passing year. Fairly quick growing, it's stiffly ascending branches form a narrow but large conical crown even at maturity. It shows fine autumn colours and thrives best on free draining soils.

Mature height: 5-10m | Shape of mature tree | Bark interest

Telephone 01353 720 748 • www.barcham.co.uk • Fax 01353 723 060   207

# PRUNUS serrula Tibetica
## *Tibetan Cherry*

This lovely cherry was introduced from Western China in 1908 by Ernest Wilson and is surely one of the best trees available for bark interest. Available as single stemmed or multi-stemmed this wonderfully dramatic tree can provide great contrast within a garden or urban environment. Its many horticultural honours culminated in the Award of Garden Merit in 2002.

| 5\|10 | Shape of mature tree | Multi-stem | Bark interest |
| Mature height: 5-10m | | | |

A fast growing, but small tree of rounded form. It has really shiny, mahogany-brown bark that just keeps on getting better and more sensational with age which makes it worth growing for this reason alone. It has narrow, willow-like leaves and small, white flowers, which are produced in April. Like most cherries it thrives best on free draining soils.

# PRUNUS Shimidsu Sakura

This dainty Japanese Cherry, introduced very early in the 1900s is also known as Shôgetsu. It is remarkably pretty in flower and in my opinion the most attractive flowering cherry on the market although Prunus Shirofugen comes a close second! A First Class Certificate winner in 1989 it also won the Award of Garden Merit.

A small tree with a broad, rounded habit, this is one of the most outstanding Japanese Cherries, and one we strongly recommend for verges, parks and gardens.  The pink buds open to reveal large, white, petals sharply toothed at the fringe, which clothe the branches in long stalked clusters.

Mature height: 5-10m    Shape of mature tree    Flowering trees

# PRUNUS Shirotae

This cherry is sometimes referred to as Mount Fuji and was introduced to Britain in the early 1900s. Like most weeping varieties it gets better with age and at maturity it can be overwhelmingly stunning when seen in full flower against a blue spring sky. It won the Award of Garden Merit in 2002.

Gently weeping is perhaps the best way to describe the habit of this small, but vigorous tree.  Green fringed foliage is followed by very large single and semi-double pure white flowers.  Very good for verges, parks and gardens.

Mature height: 5-10m    Shape of mature tree    Flowering trees

# PRUNUS Shirofugen

**A late and long lasting flowerer introduced in the very early 1900s by Ernest Wilson that won the Award of Garden Merit in 2002. Considered by many as the best flowering cherry on the market, it is hard to disagree with them. A superb garden tree, it also thrives within an urban environment.**

A rather spreading tree with a rounded crown, Shirofugen remains small. Its large, double, white flowers finish pink, contrasting well with the young, copper coloured foliage. Excellent for verges, parks and gardens it is a wonderful sight when in full flow. It thrives best on free draining soils. Its floral display is incredibly long lasting.

5|10
Mature height:
5-10m

Shape of
mature tree

Flowering
trees

● Telephone 01353 720 748  ● www.barcham.co.uk  ● Fax 01353 723 060

# PRUNUS x subhirtella Autumnalis

## *Autumn Cherry*

The Autumn Cherry brings cheer at the darkest time of year. Introduced in 1894 it won the Award of Merit in 1930 and remains a favourite for planting in the UK. Often top grafted on the continent, we strongly recommend base grafted trees for structural longevity.

This small, rounded tree produces its semi-double, white flowers intermittently from November through to March – a welcome sight on a bleak, winter's day. Autumn foliage is orange-yellow. A lovely tree for streets, parks and gardens that thrives best on well drained soils.

5|10 Mature height: 5-10m | Shape of mature tree | Flowering trees

# PRUNUS x subhirtella Autumnalis Rosea

An alternative form of the beautiful Autumn Cherry that won the Award of Garden Merit in 2002 after it received the Award of Merit in 1960. Prized by inventive flower arrangers in winter for its woody flowering stems.

5|10 Mature height: 5-10m | Shape of mature tree | Flowering trees

This small, rounded tree produces its semi-double, pink flowers sporadically from November through to March – a welcome sight in the dark, winter months. Autumn foliage is orange-yellow. Ideal for streets, parks or gardens but it does not care for waterlogged ground.

P

## PRUNUS x subhirtella Pendula

Raised in Japan and introduced to the UK in 1862, this lovely cherry won the Award of Merit in 1930. It makes a great garden tree that requires little maintenance so it is strange that it is not readily available from many nurseries.

It forms a dainty small tree with a pendulous habit similar to Betula pendula Youngii. Tiny pale pink flowers in spring add to its appeal. Like all cherries, avoid water logged soils or soils prone to lying wet over winter.

Mature height: 5-10m | Shape of mature tree | Flowering trees

## PRUNUS Sunset Boulevard

This relatively new introduction was bred at the Arboretum Kalmthout, Belgium, in the late 1980s for urban use. Many state it is extremely columnar but we reckon broadly oval would be more appropriate a description.

**Its young coppery foliage turns green in summer and golden yellow in autumn and its large, white, single flowers are edged with pink. This durable tree is very good for parks and street plantings and thrives best on free draining soils.**

Mature height: 10-15m | Shape of mature tree | Flowering trees

# PRUNUS Taihaku

## *Great White Cherry*

The Great White Cherry makes a magnificent specimen. The famous cherry enthusiast, Captain Collingwood Ingram, reintroduced this fine tree back to its native Japan in 1932 after he found a specimen growing in a Sussex garden. A winner of numerous awards including the First Class Certificate in 1944, the Award of Merit in 1931 and the Award of Garden Merit in 2002.

### Great White Cherry

One of the finest of all Cherries, and probably the best of the "whites", it bears its large, single flowers profusely, contrasting beautifully with its young, copper coloured foliage. Very good for urban plantings, streets, parks and gardens, but in our experience it does not thrive in very wet soils. It is of medium height and rounded habit.

Like many flowering cherries its best moments are demonstrated mainly in the spring and early summer but this relatively short display still makes planting this clone well worth the endeavour. Its foliage can turn to a beautiful yellow / orange in the autumn. Never accept a top grafted plant as they are prone to a shorter life expectancy.

| 10|15 | | |
|---|---|---|
| Mature height: 10-15m | Shape of mature tree | Flowering trees |

# PRUNUS Ukon

Introduced in the early 1900s this unusual cherry won the Award of Garden Merit in 2002. Sometimes imported as top grafted from the continent. This is a false economy in the long term, as the top can outgrow the bottom. We would advise base grafted trees.

A vigorous, rounded, medium size tree with a rather spreading crown, it has unusual pale yellow flowers, tinged with green and occasionally flushed with pink. They are semi-double and work well with the young bronze foliage. Its large green leaves produce a great autumn display of red and purple.

Mature height: 5-10m

Shape of mature tree

Flowering trees

# PRUNUS Umineko

**This Flowering Cherry is a cross between Prunus incisa and Prunus speciosa. Sometimes also referred to as 'Snow Goose' it won the Award of Merit in 1928 and represents a very good tree for the urban environment.**

Umineko has a narrow, columnar form, which broadens with age and is a very good choice for streets, parks, gardens and other restricted areas. It makes a medium size tree, and its white, single flowers are produced in April, along with the foliage, which colours very well in autumn. It is a robust and vigorous tree that thrives best on free draining soils.

Mature height: 5-10m

Shape of mature tree

Flowering trees

# PRUNUS virginiana Schubert

This Choke Cherry has been in cultivation since the 1950s. Its native origins in the States derive from a shrubby suckering tree and unfortunately this can be true of Schubert.

A small, conical tree, the young foliage of which quickly turns from green to a rich red-purple. It bears small, white flowers in May and dark red fruits later in the year. Be prepared to keep on top of the suckering on this one!

Mature height: 5-10m

Shape of mature tree

Red/purple foliage

Telephone 01353 720 748   •   www.barcham.co.uk   •   Fax 01353 723 060

# PRUNUS x yedoensis

## *Yoshino Cherry*

The Yoshino Cherry is a cross between Prunus speciosa and Prunus x subhirtella. It came from Japan around 1902 and won the Award of Garden Merit in 2002. This superbly pretty tree is hard to beat when in full flow and there is a particularly nice specimen to behold at Kew Gardens.

A broad, flat crowned tree, its arching branches create an almost weeping effect. It is of medium height and puts on a wonderful display of almond-scented, blush-white blossom in late March and early April. The fruits are dark red, almost black. Lovely as a park tree and also very good on broad verges.

| Mature height: 5-10m | Shape of mature tree | Flowering trees |

# PTEROCARYA fraxinifolia

## *Wing Nut*

The Wing Nut, a relative of the Walnut originating from Iran, was introduced into the UK way back in 1782. It is a brute of a tree with some specimens reaching over 38 metres high with a crown diameter of 35 metres so be sure to give it enough room!

A fast growing, large and broadly oval tree, which does well in most fertile, moisture-retentive soils, but is especially good for use close to rivers and lakes in parkland setting. It has deeply furrowed bark and very long summer catkins, which produce two-winged nut fruits. Its deciduous dark green leaves can be up to 60 cm long and separated by numerous toothed leaflets.

| Mature height: 20m+ | Shape of mature tree | Parkland trees |

# PYRUS Beurre Hardy

**A strong growing pear, grown at Barcham as a full standard and a vigorous cropper that is particularly valued by our staff in September!**

This small, rounded tree does best in a warm, sunny, sheltered position, such as a courtyard garden. The large fruits, greenish yellow flushed with red, are juicy and have a distinctive flavour. They are best picked while still hard and allowed to ripen in store. The foliage turns bright red in autumn.

| Mature height: 5-10m | Shape of mature tree | Edible fruits |

# PYRUS calleryana Chanticleer

This Ornamental Pear was selected in the USA and named after the cockerel in Chaucer's Canterbury Tales. Bred by Edward Scanlon and patented in the States in 1965, it is often referred to as the 'Bradford Pear' which is in fact slightly broader and denser.

It won the Award of Garden Merit in 2002 and as its green lush foliage is so early to appear in spring and so late to fall in autumn it has excellent screening uses.

It is one of the very best Ornamental Pears with much to recommend it. It is of medium height, generally rather columnar, becoming more oval when mature. Abundant blossom is produced as early as March, followed by glossy foliage which is late to fall in autumn, when it turns orange and red. It has rapidly established itself as a fine street tree, and is tolerant of air pollution and even salty, coastal winds. An excellent choice for the urban or rural environments.

10|15
Mature height:
10-15m

Shape of
mature tree

Urban
trees

● Telephone 01353 720 748  ● www.barcham.co.uk  ● Fax 01353 723 060

# PYRUS calleryana Redspire

**Patented by Princeton Nursery in America in 1975, this seedling of Bradford Pear is happily less vigorous than its parent which has been known to break apart when older due to tight branch angles. As the foliage is so late to fall in autumn it is also great for screening.**

Similar in many ways to Chanticleer, but Redspire has rather better autumn colour. It is of medium height, generally rather columnar, becoming more oval when mature.  Profuse white blossom is produced in spring, followed by glossy foliage which becomes orange and red.  An excellent choice for urban conditions and very good in streets and gardens.

|  |  |  |
|---|---|---|
| 10\|15 Mature height: 10-15m | Shape of mature tree | Autumn colour |

# PYRUS communis Beech Hill

Many nurseries describe this as a splendid upright variety requiring little maintenance but most fail to mention the volume of fruit produced by late summer that weigh the stiffly ascending branches down. The small fruits are not edible and very hard so not ideal for urban plantings.

This medium size tree has a columnar form when young, but opens out as it matures.  It provides good spring interest with its white flowers and shiny green leaves that turn to attractive shades of orange and red in autumn.  Best suited to gardens.

| 10\|15 Mature height: 10-15m | Shape of mature tree | Garden trees |
|---|---|---|

# PYRUS communis Conference

*Conference Pear*

First introduced in 1885, this well known eating pear variety won the Award of Garden Merit in 2002. Grown at Barcham as a full standard tree for garden planting.

Juicy and sweet green / yellow fruits are generally ready October through to November. This cultivar partially self pollinates and is a good pollinator of other varieties. It tolerates most soil conditions and is still the nation's favoured edible pear.

| 5\|7 Mature height: 5-7m | Shape of mature tree | Edible fruits |
|---|---|---|

# PYRUS Doyenne du Comice

*Commice Pear*

Introduced from France in 1849 this tasty pear requires a pollinator and produces yellow / green rotund fruits that can be harvested from late September.

Not as well cultivated as Conference, it has more flavour but less storage longevity. It won the Award of Garden Merit in 2002 and is worth planting alongside Pyrus communis Beech Hill which can act as the pollinator. Like most fruit trees we recommend a metre radius mulch ring round each tree to promote fruit size and to avoid planting in soils with poor drainage.

Mature height: 3-7m | Shape of mature tree | Edible fruits

# PYRUS salicifolia Pendula

*Willow-Leaved Pear*

This very popular garden tree won the Award of Garden Merit in 2002. Its dainty foliage can provide lovely contrast and the tree is very adaptable in that I have seen it pruned in a variety of shapes and sizes.

This weeping and rather broad small tree produces its creamy white flowers and willow-like silvery grey foliage at the same time in spring. Its weeping branches are silver grey, giving good winter interest. A very good subject for parks and gardens tolerating urban conditions well. It reacts well to severe pruning in the early spring, just before the leaves emerge to prevent the crown getting too woody.

Mature height: 5-10m | Shape of mature tree | Garden trees

# QUERCUS castaneifolia

## *Chestnut-leaved Oak*

The Chestnut-leaved Oak was introduced from the Caucasus and Iran in the mid 1840s but is rarely seen in the UK. A must for any plant collector who has the space to plant one.

Similar to Quercus cerris in appearance, this medium to large, oval shaped tree has oblong leaves, tapered at both ends. It is a magnificent tree for parks, arboretums and woodlands where there is space for its superb crown to mature.

Mature height: 15-20m

Shape of mature tree

Parkland trees

# QUERCUS cerris

## *Turkey Oak*

The highly durable Turkey Oak was introduced into the UK in 1735. A magnificent specimen can be seen at the National Trust's Knightshayes Garden in Devon, where it imposes itself on the field in which it stands.

This large, rounded tree is probably the fastest growing Oak grown in Britain. It does well even in chalky soils and in coastal areas. The dark green, lobed leaves are resistant to mildew, which affects some others of the genus. A tough tree, good for wide verges and parks.

Mature height: 20m+

Shape of mature tree

Parkland trees

● Telephone 01353 720 748  ● www.barcham.co.uk  ● Fax 01353 723 060

# QUERCUS coccinea

## *Scarlet Oak*

**This superb autumn colourer was introduced from its native South Eastern Canada and Eastern USA in 1691. The USA national champion in Kentucky is over 40 metres tall by 31 metres wide but trees of this stature are only seen on dry sandy soils which suits it best.**

It requires a slightly acidic soil to perform at its best, so select the more robust Quercus palustris if in doubt. The overall effect is very similar.

Mature height: 20m+ | Shape of mature tree | Parkland trees

A large and impressive subject, with a broad and rounded habit. The summer's dark, glossy, green leaves turn, branch by branch, to a flaming scarlet as autumn progresses. Its acorns are carried in shallow cups.

A magnificent specimen for planting in parkland but it is often confused in the UK with Quercus Palustris.

# QUERCUS frainetto

## *Hungarian Oak*

This stately tree was introduced from South East Europe in the late 1830s. There are some magnificent specimens at the National Trust's Anglesey Abbey in Cambridgeshire which coincidentally is a garden not to be missed if you are in the vicinity!

This is a large tree with a broad, rounded crown. Its fissured bark and large, dark green leaves, which are boldly cut and regularly lobed, makes this a most striking subject for parks and woodlands. We also recommend it as an avenue tree. It does best on moist soils, but will tolerate chalky ones. The clone "Trump" retains a slightly improved shape at maturity.

Mature height: 20m+ | Shape of mature tree | Parkland trees

# QUERCUS hispanica Wageningen

**This rarely seen tree is thought to be a hybrid between Quercus Castaneifolia and Quercus Lucombeana and is furnished with green glossy leaves that are beyond 10cm in length and 5cm across.**

An interesting addition to parkland planting as this clone generally hangs onto its leaves until the spring. It has an upright habit when young and broadens with age to develop into a large tree with a rough bark at maturity. It thrives on most fertile soils.

| 15\|20 | | |
|---|---|---|
| Mature height: 15-20m | Shape of mature tree | Parkland trees |

# QUERCUS ilex

*Holm Oak*

The Holm Oak is a native of Mediterranean countries, but it has been grown in Britain since the 1500s, and is now thought to be a native of Southern Ireland. The timber is hard and long-lasting, used for joinery, vine-props and for charcoal. It won the Award of Garden Merit in 2002 and is surely one of the most majestic of evergreen trees grown in the UK.

| 20+ | | |
|---|---|---|
| Mature height: 20m+ | Shape of mature tree | Evergreen trees |

If left to its own devices it forms a large tree with a densely rounded habit, good examples of which can be seen opposite Holkham Hall on the North Norfolk coast. It is perhaps surprisingly versatile, being suitable for coastal plantings, topiary and as stilted hedging. It also tolerates shade and air pollution. Suitable for parks and gardens but thriving best on free draining soils.

# QUERCUS imbricaria

## *Shingle Oak*

The Shingle Oak was introduced from North America in the 1780s. Its name derives from its use for roof tiles "shingles" in its native land. The USA national champion is in Ohio and stands at over 35 metres in height with a crown at over 23 metres across, so it is not for the faint-hearted!

A medium to large vigorous tree, it has a pyramidal habit, and shiny dark green leaves,which turn golden in the autumn. Splendid for parks or estates, it thrives best on moist but well drained deep fertile acid soils and prefers full sun.

Mature height: 20m+ | Shape of mature tree | Parkland trees

# QUERCUS palustris

## *Pin Oak*

More pyramidal at maturity than the similar Quercus coccinea, this magnificent tree was introduced into the UK from its native North America in 1800. It is a relatively tough tree and can withstand limited periods of water logging even though it prefers free draining slightly acidic soils. The USA national champion is in Tennessee and stands at 37 metres tall and broad. It won the Award of Garden Merit in 2002.

This large, pyramidal tree is one of the most graceful of Oaks, with its slender branches gently drooping at their tips. Its autumn colour is simply stunning.

Mature height: 20m+ | Shape of mature tree | Parkland trees

# QUERCUS petraea

## *Sessile Oak*

One of our two native Oaks, the Sessile Oak is long-lived and was extensively used in ship-building. A winner of the Award of Garden Merit in 2002 it is more often seen on the west side of the UK where rainfall is higher.

**A good choice for coastal locations, this large, oval shaped tree will also tolerate acid soils. Similar in many respects to Quercus robur, it tends to have a greater degree of apical dominance so developing a more pyramidal crown. A wonderful choice for wildlife, this tree supports a host of animals.**

Mature height: 20m+ | Shape of mature tree | Parkland trees

# QUERCUS robur

## *Common Oak, English Oak*

Perhaps the most majestic of our native trees, the English or Common Oak was once the predominant species in English lowland forests, and has become virtually a national emblem. Very long-lived, its hard timber has been used to produce the finest furniture, from ships through to coffins.

Many superb specimens exist in our countryside but perhaps the most famous is the Major Oak in Sherwood Forest which is estimated to be some 1000 years old and weigh over 23 tonnes. Whether Robin Hood actually took refuge in it is of debate!

## *English Oak*

A large, imposing, broadly oval tree, heavy-limbed and long-lived. Its deeply grained bark gives year-round appeal, and its expansive root system does best on deep, heavy soils.

A wonderful choice for parkland and large estates, it is also good in avenues and wide verges. It is a great host for supporting wildlife and its acorns are hidden and distributed by forgetful Jays. Given the right conditions one can expect between three and four summer flushes of growth.

| 20+ | | |
|---|---|---|
| Mature height: 20m+ | Shape of mature tree | Parkland trees |

# QUERCUS robur Fastigiata (Koster)

## *Cypress Oak*

The Cypress Oak used to be seed grown, which resulted in variability in its form, so now the industry standard is the uniformly narrow clone 'Koster' which is grafted onto Quercus robur rootstock. It won the Award of Garden Merit in 2002.

Common Oak is such a wonderful tree for wildlife, that for restricted areas this clone makes it possible to plant one. It thrives best in more rural environments where soil volumes are greater to support its growth.

| 15\|20 | Shape of | Narrow |
| Mature height: 15-20m | mature tree | trees |

# QUERCUS rubra

## *Red Oak*

Introduced from its native North America in 1724, this well known stately tree won the Award of Merit in 1971 and the updated Award of Garden Merit in 2002. The bark of the Red Oak is rich in tannin – essential for tanning leather.

This large, broadly oval tree does best in deep fertile soils, but tolerates most others. It is a fast grower and seems to tolerate polluted air well. Young growth emerges almost yellow in the spring before expanding into large broad green and lobed leaves by May. These in turn go a wonderful red in autumn before tuning a red / brown and falling. Best suited for planting in parks and large gardens.

| 20+ | Shape of | Parkland |
| Mature height: 20m+ | mature tree | trees |

● Telephone 01353 720 748 ● www.barcham.co.uk ● Fax 01353 723 060

# QUERCUS suber

*Cork Oak*

Introduced in the late 1690s, the Cork Oak is a native of southern Europe and North Africa so in the UK it is best suited to the warmer south. Until it gets beyond semi-mature it is often buoyed up by a thick bamboo cane by nurseries to support the weak stem. Our advice is never accept one unless it is strong enough to support itself.

**Widely grown in Spain and Portugal for the wine industry it is resistant to British frosts. It is a short stemmed, wide, rounded, evergreen tree. Its thick and craggy bark can provide outstanding interest in a garden and it tends to thrive better on free draining soils.**

Mature height: 5-10m

Shape of mature tree

Garden trees

# RHUS typhina

*Stag's Horn Sumach*

Stag's Horn Sumach can be grown as a small tree or as a shrub. A native of North America, it was introduced into the UK in the late 1620s and won the Award of Garden Merit in 2002. It may surprise you that the national champion in the States is over 20 metres tall but I have not seen one much over 5 metres over here.

Mature height: 5-10m

Shape of mature tree

Garden trees

This small tree has an irregular wide spreading and rather architectural habit. It provides superb autumn colour, and the conical red fruit clusters last for much of the winter. Very good for gardens and parks. It can be prone to suckering so allow for this when planning its position.

# ROBINIA pseudoacacia

*False Acacia*

The False Acacia was introduced to France from America in 1601, and is now naturalised through much of Europe. It produces large epicormic thorns and can be prone to suckering so it can be used as a stout defence against unwelcome visitors.

A large irregular crowned tree with soft, green, pinnate leaves that emerge early May. Racemes of sweetly scented white flowers in June are replaced by purple tinged seed pods in autumn. It thrives on any soil, and tolerates urban pollution, but is not good in windy, exposed locations due to its rather brittle branches.

Mature height: 10-15m

Shape of mature tree

Parkland trees

# ROBINIA pseudoacacia Bessoniana

**This thornless clone, in cultivation since the 1870s, can be seen at its mature dimensions in the Royal Horticultural Garden at Wisely. It seldom flowers and its foliage is a paler but more vibrant green that its parent.**

Of only medium height, this clone is probably the best Robinia cultivar for street planting. It has a compact, rounded crown of virtually thorn-free branches and pale green leaves. It thrives on any soil, and tolerates urban pollution, but its brittle and twiggy growth is not suited to windy sites.

Mature height: 10-15m

Shape of mature tree

Urban trees

# ROBINIA pseudoacacia Casque Rouge

This delightful cultivar of False Acacia makes a particularly fine garden, verge or parkland tree as its profuse flowers emerge in June after the Cherries, Crab Apples and Thorns have all finished.

This tree of medium height and broadly rounded habit is greatly prized for its showy and highly ornamental lilac-pink flowers that are richly appreciated by all those who notice. It thrives on any soil, and tolerates urban pollution, but is not good in windy, exposed locations due to its rather brittle branches.

Mature height: 10-15m

Shape of mature tree

Flowering trees

● Telephone 01353 720 748 ● www.barcham.co.uk ● Fax 01353 723 060

# ROBINIA pseudoacacia Frisia

This superb yellow clone has been very popular over the passed 25 years and can now be seen in most urban areas in the UK. It is tolerant of dry conditions and is well suited to cope with reflected heat and light from buildings and pavements. It won the Award of Garden Merit in 2002.

Raised in the Netherlands in the mid 1930s, this medium tree of rounded habit only rarely flowers, but displays its beautiful golden yellow foliage from spring through to autumn. It thrives on any soil, and tolerates urban pollution.

10-15m

Shape of mature tree

Garden trees

# ROBINIA pseudoacacia Umbraculifera

**In cultivation since the early 1800s this top grafted clone forms a rounded and compact crown ideal for urban piazzas and town gardens. It is more regularly seen in French and German cities than here in the UK.**

This small, mop-headed tree seldom flowers and requires very little maintenance. The largest tree of this clone I have heard of is about 6 metres in diameter. It is best to have them top grafted between 1.8-2 metres from ground level so they can easily be walked under. It thrives on most soils and is tolerant of urban conditions.

Mature height: 5-10m

Shape of mature tree

Urban trees

# ROBINIA pseudoacacia Fastigiata

This rather curious and unusual False Acacia was introduced in the early 1840s and is sometimes referred to as 'Pyramidalis'. Best suited to sheltered gardens or urban courtyards, it is a slow growing slender tree that can be very useful for planting into areas where space is at a premium.

The branch unions can grow with included bark and for Robinia, which are brittle at the best of times, this can be problematical, and so our advice is to not plant on exposed sites. It thrives on most soils, and tolerates urban pollution.

| 5\|10 | | |
| Mature height: 5-10m | Shape of mature tree | Garden trees |

# SALIX alba
*White Willow*

Our native White Willow is a lovely subject for water-side plantings. Very prominent in our fenland landscape surrounding the nursery, it reacts well to regular pollarding where size becomes an issue.

A fast growing, large, conical tree with slender branches which droop at the tips. The leaves give a characteristically silver appearance from a distance. Catkins are borne in spring. Although it is good in wet soils and will tolerate temporary flooding, it thrives in most soils, and is a fine choice for coastal areas.

| 20+ | | |
| Mature height: 20m+ | Shape of mature tree | Native trees |

● Telephone 01353 720 748   ● www.barcham.co.uk   ● Fax 01353 723 060

# SALIX alba Chermesina

## *Scarlet Willow*

This clone is also known by the cultivar name of Britzensis. A winner of the Award of Garden Merit in 2002, it has been known to extend over 3 metres of growth in a single growing season from a coppice.

A medium to large tree with a rather pyramidal crown, its young branches are a brilliant orange-red in winter, especially if severely pruned every other year to produce a multi-stemmed tree. It makes a very good park tree and thrives on most soils including those prone to flooding.

 Mature height: 15-20m
 Shape of mature tree
 Wet soils

# SALIX alba Liempde

This male clone has been planted extensively in the Netherlands, where it was selected in the late 1960s. As with all willows it reacts well to pruning if its ultimate size is too much to handle and this work is best undertaken in the winter months.

**This vigorous tree has upright branches which form a narrow, conical tree. The slender, silvery green leaves turn clear yellow in autumn. It does particularly well in wet soils, and is suited to coastal areas.**

 Mature height: 20m+
 Shape of mature tree
 Wet soils

# SALIX alba Tristis (Chrysocoma)

*Golden Willow*

The beautiful and much admired Weeping Willow has several botanical names including Salix babylonica and Salix vitellina Pendula but in fact is a hybrid of the two with a bit of Salix alba thrown in for good measure. A winner of the Award of Garden Merit in 2002 this is surely one of the most graceful weeping trees grown in the UK.

Mature height: 20m+

Shape of mature tree

Wet soils

## Golden Willow

It is a large, weeping and wide spreading tree, often seen close to water as it does so well in wet soils. The narrow, pale green leaves are early to flush in the spring and slow to fall in the autumn. A fast grower well suited to parks. It reacts well to severe crown pruning sending the glorious golden stems and light green foliage plunging towards the ground.

# SALIX caprea
*Pussy Willow*

The Pussy Willow has been loved by generations of children, and is often associated with Easter. Sometimes referred to as Goat Willow, it is a tough prospect for industrial areas that need rapid greening.

One of our native Willows, this makes a small, rounded tree and is often found by rivers and streams, as it thrives in damp soil. It is particularly noted for its silver-white, furry catkins, which open to yellow in spring.

5|10 Mature height: 5-10m — Shape of mature tree — Wet soils

# SALIX caprea Pendula
*Kilmarnock Willow*

**The weeping form of Pussy Willow that is top grafted onto a Salix caprea stem. It was discovered by the side of the River Ayr in Scotland in the mid 1850s and was awarded the Award of Merit in 1977.**

This small male weeping tree, which does best on moist soils, is perfect for gardens, producing the ultimate shape resembling an umbrella. Its yellow shoots are followed in spring by attractive, grey catkins.

3|5 Mature height: 3-5m — Shape of mature tree — Garden trees

# SALIX daphnoides
*Violet Willow*

Native to Northern Europe, Central Asia and the Himalayas, this lovely tree was introduced into the UK in the late 1820s and won the Award of Merit in 1957. The Violet Willow is an excellent choice for coppicing to show off its sensational purple-violet shoots overlaid with a white bloom.

Catkins are an attractive feature in spring. This is a medium, fast growing tree with a rounded habit that thrives on most soils including wet ones. The male clone 'Aglaia' is often grown by nurseries for ease of propagation but its properties are the same.

10|15 Mature height: 10-15m — Shape of mature tree — Wet soils

# SALIX matsudana Tortuosa

## *Dragon's Claw Willow*

**Introduced from its native China in 1905, the fondly known 'Wiggerly Willow' is otherwise known as Salix babylonica Pekinensis, the Pekin Willow.**

A weird and wonderful sight in winter when its framework of contorted and twisted branches can be best appreciated. It is a fast growing, medium to large tree with a rounded habit. Good for parks, garden and for waterside plantings, it is also prized by flower arrangers and by my wife to hang Easter decorations.

| 10\|15 | | |
|---|---|---|
| Mature height: 10-15m | Shape of mature tree | Garden trees |

# SALIX pentandra

## *Bay Willow*

The native Bay Willow is sometimes found growing wild in northern areas of Britain and developed its name from the Norwegians who use it as a substitute for tender Laurus nobilis as its foliage is pleasantly aromatic when crushed.

A most beautiful, medium size tree with a rounded crown at maturity. Catkins are produced at the same time as the leaves in late spring.

| 10\|15 | | |
|---|---|---|
| Mature height: 10-15m | Shape of mature tree | Wet soils |

Very good for parks and wetland areas, it is both vigorous and vibrant. It is often overlooked by specifiers but is a lovely native tree that could be used more often. This tree is always a good one to throw into the mix on a plant identification competition as it tends to catch a lot of people out.

Telephone 01353 720 748 • www.barcham.co.uk • Fax 01353 723 060

# SEQUOIADENDRON giganteum
## *Wellingtonia*

The Wellingtonia is a native of California, where it grows incredibly tall on the western slopes of the Sierra Nevada and can live for more than 3000 years. It holds the distinction of being the largest living thing on Earth.

Introduced into the UK in the early 1890s, it is quick to grow and there are a number of fine examples growing today including the collection at Wakehurst Place in Sussex. The USA national champion is in Sequoia National Park and stands at a staggering 92 metres tall by 36 metres wide.

Mature height: 20m+

Shape of mature tree

Evergreen trees

## *Wellingtonia*

A large, evergreen conifer, it has a densely branched, conical habit while young, but the branches become more widely spaced and distinctly down swept as it ages. Its deeply furrowed, red-brown bark is another of the hallmarks of this magnificent specimen, which is suited to large country estates and parklands. It thrives on most soils and romps away when young given enough water.

# SEQUOIA sempervirens
## *Coastal Redwood*

The Coastal Redwood first came to Europe (St Petersburg) from California in 1840. You cannot help but be touched by the majesty of these trees as you head through California to Oregon on the coastal road into the Valley of the Giants. Even my young children were awestruck at the beauty and sheer magnitude of these trees!

A large, conical evergreen, it has a thick, fibrous, red-brown outer bark, which is soft and spongy to the touch. The slightly drooping branches bear two-ranked, linear-oblong leaves. A wonderful choice for large areas of parkland, they prefer the cleaner air of rural sites and plenty of water to get them going.

Mature height: 20m+

Shape of mature tree

Evergreen trees

Sequoia sempervirens

# SOPHORA japonica
## *Japanese Pagoda Tree*

Introduced in 1753 this heat loving tree won the Award of Garden Merit in 2002 but truthfully is only worth while in the warmer parts of Southern England on south facing sites. Despite its specific and common names, this medium to large, rounded tree is actually a native of China, although widely planted in Japan.

**Once mature, panicles of yellow-white, pea like flowers are borne in August, followed by long grey seed pods in autumn. The clone 'Princeton Upright' is so like its parents to be of any consequence.**

Mature height: 10-15m

Shape of mature tree

Garden trees

● Telephone 01353 720 748  ● www.barcham.co.uk  ● Fax 01353 723 060

# SORBUS aria Lutescens

**This outstanding clone is most attractive in spring and won the Award of Merit in 1952 and the Award of Garden Merit in 2002. A very popular choice for urban gardens, it requires little maintenance and tolerates chalk soils.**

The young leaves emerge silvery-white from purple shoots in spring, before hardening to grey-green in summer. This is a small, compact, rounded tree, producing white flowers in April and May and, in good years, orange-red, cherry like fruits in autumn. A very good choice for streets, gardens and parks.

7|10
Mature height: 7-10m

Shape of mature tree

Garden trees

# SORBUS aria Magnifica

Introduced into general nursery cultivation in the early 1920s, this urban clone has ascending branches and is well equipped to cope with the rigours of reflected heat and light common to developed areas. Although it is not as stunning in the spring as 'Lutescens' it will keep going for longer in the late summer and autumn.

This medium size tree is conical when young, becoming broadly oval at maturity. The large leaves are dark green on top, with silver-white undersides. It has the white flowers and red fruits characteristic of the species, and is a good choice for parks, streets and avenues.

10|15
Mature height: 10-15m

Shape of mature tree

Urban trees

# SORBUS aria
# Majestica

This well known variety is also known as Decaisneana and won the Award of Garden Merit in 2002. In our opinion this clone is synonymous to 'Magnifica' for its overall effect and thrives on most soils including chalky ones.

A tree of medium height with a broad, dense, conical crown, it is of symmetrical form. It has notably large leaves and fruits, and is a splendid choice for parks, streets, gardens and avenues. For further Whitebeam types, refer to Sorbus latifolia and intermedia.

| 10|15 | Shape of | Urban |
| Mature height: 10-15m | mature tree | trees |

# SORBUS aria Mitchellii

This clone with its huge leaves is beautiful when lit from underneath, as demonstrated in the churchyard opposite The George Hotel of Stamford in Lincolnshire. A winner of the Award of Garden Merit in 2002 it is sometimes classified as Sorbus thibetica John Mitchell.

**This small tree with a rounded habit has dark green leaves with white undersides that can get up to 15cm long and broad. A great tree to provide contrast in a garden environment and it thrives on most free draining soils.**

| 7|10 | Shape of | Garden |
| Mature height: 7-10m | mature tree | trees |

Telephone 01353 720 748  •  www.barcham.co.uk  •  Fax 01353 723 060

# SORBUS x arnoldiana Schouten

A reliable, low-maintenance Mountain Ash clone that has proved to be a very popular choice for street planting in London. Unlike many rowan types, it tolerates the reflected heat and light thrown up by hard urban areas.

Budded onto Sorbus aucuparia rootstock, this is a great choice for streets, car parks and urban plantings, because it needs next to no maintenance. It is a small tree with a dense, oval crown, and it has most attractive, green, feathery foliage with golden yellow berries from August onwards.

| | | |
|---|---|---|
| 7\|10 | | |
| Mature height: 7-10m | Shape of mature tree | Urban trees |

# SORBUS aucuparia

*Rowan/Mountain Ash*

This wonderful native tree is often associated with Scotland. It certainly suits bird life as the profuse red autumn berries provide a lot of autumnal sustenance.

We grow this multi-stemmed rather than in standard form as they are not regular in shape and it is better to opt for a clone such as Rossica Major if uniformity is required. Rowans prefer shorter day lengths and do not thrive in areas with excessive reflective heat and light such as paved and other hard surfaces. Best planted in parkland or verges, it is arguably our prettiest native tree.

| | | | |
|---|---|---|---|
| 10\|15 | | | |
| Mature height: 10-15m | Shape of mature tree | Multi-stem | Native trees |

# SORBUS aucuparia Asplenifolia

**This Rowan clone is also sometimes referred to as 'Laciniata' and has proved very popular for both urban and rural planting. There are very few cut leaf trees and their addition into the landscape provides lovely foliage contrast.**

Highly recommended for streets, verges and garden planting, this medium tree forms a broad pyramid if the leader is retained.  It has finely cut, fern like foliage, which turns orange-red in autumn and the red berries are loved by wild birds.  Rowans readily thrive on most soils including acid ones.

Mature height: 10-15m

Shape of mature tree

Garden trees

# SORBUS aucuparia Cardinal Royal

Introduced by Michigan State University in America, their original plant stands at 12 metres tall by 6 metres wide. This makes it a very good Rowan clone for restricted areas and it is also tolerant of the reflected heat and light associated with urban planting.

The ascending branches of this medium size tree give it a columnar habit at maturity.  White flowers in May are followed by red berries in September, which are readily consumed by wild birds.  Very good for streets, gardens, urban plantings and gardens. It will thrive on most soils including acid ones.

Mature height: 10-15m

Shape of mature tree

Urban trees

Telephone 01353 720 748   •   www.barcham.co.uk   •   Fax 01353 723 060

# SORBUS aucuparia Edulis

The edible berries of this Mountain Ash can be used to make Rowan jelly. Thought to have been introduced in the very early 1800s, it is sometimes also classified under the varietal names 'Moravica' or 'Dulcis'.

A vigorous and very hardy tree, which is of medium size and broadly oval at maturity. It has larger leaves than the species – and large berries too. A good choice for gardens and urban areas, it thrives on most soils.

Mature height: 10-15m

Shape of mature tree

Garden trees

# SORBUS aucuparia Golden Wonder

Sometimes classified under the Sorbus arnoldiana group this stocky vigorous rowan makes a fine tree that requires little maintenance. Its lush leaves can turn to a decent orange / red in the autumn before falling.

**This pyramidal grower is a good choice for verges, avenues and streets. It makes a medium size, large leaved tree, which produces big bunches of golden yellow fruits from late summer onwards. It thrives on most soils but like all rowans will prefer it slightly acid.**

Mature height: 10-15m

Shape of mature tree

Urban trees

# SORBUS aucuparia Joseph Rock

One of the prettiest of rowans it is both a winner of the First Class Certificate in 1962 and the Award of Merit in 1950. However, it is also the one most susceptible to fire blight which can disfigure the tree to the point of complete demise.

Small narrow green leaflets turn a fantastic red in the autumn and provide a stunning contrast to the creamy yellow berries. A small tree with ascending branches, ideal for gardens. It derives from the Chinese species, has red leaf buds and a dainty overall effect. It is ideal for small gardens and tolerant of most soils.

Mature height: 5-10m

Shape of mature tree

Garden trees

# SORBUS aucuparia Rossica Major

As trees derived from seed grown Sorbus aucuparia are genetically unique they can be quite variable in habit so if it is uniformity you are after this clone fits the bill. Otherwise it does everything you would expect of our native rowan and requires little or no maintenance.

A strong and fast growing tree, Rossica Major forms a broadly oval crown. Its dark green leaves are attached by red stalks, and it bears its dark red berries from August onwards. A good choice for both urban areas, and rural gardens.

| Mature height: 10-15m | Shape of mature tree | Urban trees |

# SORBUS aucuparia Sheerwater Seedling

**Along with the clone 'Cardinal Royal' this variety represents the best choice for urban planting where space is restricted. A winner of the Award of garden Merit in 2002, this well known tree has proven to be popular for a number of years.**

This medium size, oval tree will also tolerate semi-shade. It thrives on most soils and its ascending branches and dominant leader makes it a tree requiring little maintenance. White flowers are followed by bird friendly red berries by September and the green leaves turn a decent yellow / orange in the autumn.

| Mature height: 10-15m | Shape of mature tree | Urban trees |

# SORBUS aucuparia Vilmorinii

Discovered by Abbe Delavay and introduced in 1889, this dainty beauty originates from Western China. It makes a lovely little tree requiring little maintenance and giving much enjoyment.

The leaves are dark green and fern-like, turning a red-purple in the autumn. Profuse berries hang in drooping clusters, dark red at first then fading to a pink-white. Unfortunately the small tree, like Joseph Rock, is also susceptible to fire blight. Ideal for small gardens.

| Mature height: 5-10m | Shape of mature tree | Garden trees |

Telephone 01353 720 748 • www.barcham.co.uk • Fax 01353 723 060

# SORBUS commixta
# Embley

*Chinese Scarlet Rowan*

Some list this as 'Embley' and some as 'commixta' but we hedge our bets and classify it as one as there is no discernable difference to the vast majority. Originating from Korea and Japan, it was introduced in the early 1880s and won the Award of Merit in 1979.

5|10
Mature height: 5-10m

Shape of mature tree

Garden trees

## Chinese Scarlet Rowan

This small tree of broadly columnar habit is tolerant of most soils and makes a fine choice for garden planting. In autumn its glorious foliage and bright red berries makes it stand out from the rest. Its young trunk is light brown and speckled. Fluffy bunches of small white flowers are produced in the spring.

# SORBUS discolor

Introduced from its native Northern China in the mid 1880s this clone is often lumped in together with 'Commixta' even though the berry colour is different. One of the earliest rowans to flower in the spring, it makes a lovely garden tree that requires little maintenance.

Creamy-yellow fruits are borne on red stalks by late summer in the manner of 'Joseph Rock' and it forms an open crown made up from ascending branches. It thrives on most soils although like most rowans it will prefer it slightly acid.

 5|10
Mature height: 5-10m

 Shape of mature tree

 Garden trees

# SORBUS hupehensis

Discovered by Ernest Wilson and introduced from its native western China in 1910, this lovely rowan stands out by its flat blue tinged leaves and light brown trunk. It won the Award of Garden Merit in 2002 and forms a compact broadly oval crown at maturity.

Splendid white berries produced in large clusters and stunning red autumn colour also typifies this small low maintenance tree which thrives on most soils and can tolerate the rigours of the urban environment. Being white, the berries are the last to be taken by birds, so can remain on the tree way passed Christmas.

Mature height:
5-10m

Shape of
mature tree

Garden
trees

# SORBUS intermedia

*Swedish Whitebeam*

The Swedish Whitebeam is widely planted as a street tree in northern Europe. It is a tough tree that can even thrive within view of the coast. Unlike the closely related Sorbus aria clones it is more tolerant of reflected heat and light bouncing of hard areas on urban sites.

A medium size tree with a well formed, rounded crown, its single, dark green leaves have silver-grey undersides. White flowers in May give way to orange-red fruits, produced in small bunches. It is wind resistant and tolerant of calcareous soils and air pollution, making this a really useful candidate for urban planting. We recommend it for streets and avenues.

Mature height:
10-15m

Shape of
mature tree

Coastal
sites

Telephone 01353 720 748 • www.barcham.co.uk • Fax 01353 723 060

# SORBUS intermedia Brouwers

This Swedish Whitebeam clone has a more pyramidal crown than the species and is more commonly grown by nurseries as the catchall for Sorbus intermedia. Clonal variations can be very similar to their parents but crucially offer a far greater degree of uniformity.

A medium size tree with a conical crown, its single, dark green leaves have silver-grey undersides. White flowers in May produce orange-red fruits. It is wind resistant and tolerant of calcareous soils and air pollution, making this a really tough tree. It will thrive in even the harshest conditions including near the coast.

| 10\|15 | | |
|---|---|---|
| Mature height: 10-15m | Shape of mature tree | Urban trees |

# SORBUS latifolia Henk Vink

A hybrid derived from Sorbus torminalis and Sorbus aria this is a Dutch clone raised for its qualities to thrive within the urban environment. A native of Portugal though to Germany, it is a worthy alternative to the more commonly used Sorbus aria clones.

**Round headed and tough, this versatile tree is ideal for streets, verges or parks. White flowers are followed by red berries in the autumn. Its leaves are grey / green and silvery grey beneath to provide a pleasing contrast in windy conditions.**

| 10\|15 | | |
|---|---|---|
| Mature height: 10-15m | Shape of mature tree | Urban trees |

# SORBUS latifolia Atrovirens
## *Service Tree of Fontainebleau*

An improved clone of the hybrid between Sorbus torminalis and aria. Native of Europe, it is seldom used due to it not being known.

Glossy lobed green leaves, grey beneath, are supported by an ascending branch network that broadens out at maturity to become rounded. White flowers in spring form orange fruits that are borne in small bunches. It is a tough tree, withstanding strong winds and coping well with urban conditions. Excellent for verge or street planting.

| 5\|10 | | |
|---|---|---|
| Mature height: 5-10m | Shape of mature tree | Urban trees |

# SORBUS x thuringiaca Fastigiata

Sometimes referred to as Sorbus hybrida, this highly useful urban tree retains the prettiness of Sorbus aucuparia and the toughness of Sorbus aria, its parents. A winner of the Award of Merit in 1924, this tree can get to beyond 10 metres if given the space. The best examples I have seen of this tree are at Calderstones Park in Liverpool, where they have been left long enough, and been given the space to express themselves.

This small tree is columnar when young, but becomes broadly oval as it matures. It is really tough and is well suited to urban plantings, withstanding air pollution very well. It is fine as a street tree and in restricted areas. Clusters of white flowers in spring are followed by bunches of red berries by September. The green / grey foliage can turn a magnificent orange in the autumn. Some recognise this as fastigiate Sorbus intermedia and overlook this clone because of its indigestible name.

7|10
Mature height:
7-10m

Shape of
mature tree

Urban
trees

● Telephone 01353 720 748  ● www.barcham.co.uk  ● Fax 01353 723 060

# SORBUS torminalis

*Wild Service Tree*

The fruits of the Wild Service Tree, which are very sharp, are edible when over-ripe, they used to be sold as "chequers" in southern England, giving rise to its alternative name of Chequer Tree and the corresponding numbers of pubs taking the same title.

This medium native tree is columnar when young, but becomes more rounded as it ages. Its dark brown, fissured bark bears grey scales. Perfect for woodlands, it thrives best under the dappled shade of others and does not react favourably to hot urban areas prone to reflected heat and light. Its attractive green lobed leaves turn a lovely orange / yellow in autumn.

Mature height: 10-15m | Shape of mature tree | Native trees

# SYRINGA vulgaris Viola

*Lilac*

**One associates Lilac as being a rather haphazard shrub but we have managed to grow this clone as a straight stem standard tree with 1.8m clear stem for street or specimen planting.**

Profuse violet flowers are produced in the spring that release a lovely fragrance into the surrounding air. It is tolerant of most soils and originated from the mountains of Eastern Europe. It readily naturalised over the rest of Europe after being introduced in the early 1600s.

Mature height: 5-7m | Shape of mature tree | Garden trees

# TAMARIX aestivalis

**A native of Europe, Asia and North Africa, this ancient looking tree is incredibly useful in exposed windy areas and will thrive on pretty much any soil apart from shallow chalk. Mostly supplied as bushes, we grow our Tamarix as full standards.**

A small genus well suited to coastal locations, tolerating salt laden winds and spray. This variety is virtually identical to Tamarix tetrandra but flowers about a month later, so by a mixed planting of both varieties you can look forward to about six weeks of continuous flower.

| Mature height: 5-10m | Shape of mature tree | Coastal sites |

# TAMARIX gallica

This coastal specialist originally from South West Europe has now naturalised along many miles of the English coastline. A great tree to tolerate and diffuse wind.

Better known as a shrub, we grow it as a full standard with a clear stem of 1.8m, best suited for coastal towns or specimen planting inland. Dark brown branches support a vivid green foliage and pink fluffy flowers in summer that are borne from new season's wood. Particularly useful on saline soils.

| Mature height: 5-7m | Shape of mature tree | Coastal sites |

# TAMARIX tetrandra

The Tamarisk is so evocative of old fashioned, Mediterranean fishing villages. Introduced way back in 1821, this won the Award of Garden Merit in 2002. Although primarily thought of as a coastal plant, it can make a fine garden tree inland, so long as it is not planted on shallow chalk.

We offer this as a small standard tree with a rounded crown. Its light pink flowers are freely produced in May / June. A tough subject, which does well in light, sandy soils. Is very good for coastal locations and is also tolerant of exposed, windy sites.

| Mature height: 5-10m | Shape of mature tree | Coastal sites |

Telephone 01353 720 748  •  www.barcham.co.uk  •  Fax 01353 723 060

# TAXODIUM distichum

## *Swamp Cypress*

The Swamp Cypress is the best conifer for wet soils. A native of the Florida Everglades, it is thought of as a pyramidal grower but interestingly the national champion in the USA is 28 metres tall by 29 metres wide suggesting seed variability. Introduced in the early 1640s by John Tradescant it won the updated Award of Garden Merit in 2002.

Foliage is always late to appear in the spring, particularly after planting, but it generally starts growing at full pelt from July onwards.

20+

Mature height: 20m+

Shape of mature tree

Wet soils

## *Swamp Cypress*

This large, deciduous, pyramidal conifer has fibrous, brown bark and small, round cones, which are purple when young. It does best in wet soils, and needs plenty of moisture in its first year after planting if it is to succeed. A good choice for parks and often confused with Metasequoia until seen close together.

# TAXUS baccata
## *English Yew*

The native English Yew is a tree of many mystical and religious associations. Incredibly long lived, the oldest reported is in Llangernyw, Wales, and is estimated to be 4000 years old with a circumference of 16 metres. The trees capacity for regeneration is outstanding; especially considering it is a conifer.

A medium tree of conical appearance, its hard wood can support this evergreen to a great age. Often used for hedging, it also makes a fine specimen tree. Very good for parks and gardens. All parts of the tree are poisonous. It can grow on highly calcareous or highly acidic soils, if there is good drainage.

10|15
Mature height: 10-15m

Shape of mature tree

Evergreen trees

# THUYA plicata Atrovirens

**A form of the Western Red Cedar. It is an important timber tree in its native North America, although it is more commonly used as a hedging conifer in the UK. The national champion in the States is over 60 metres tall by 18 metres wide. Introduced in the mid 1870s, it won the Award of Garden Merit in 2002.**

This large, evergreen conifer does best on wet soils and will tolerate shade. Of pyramidal form if grown as a specimen tree, it is also a fine subject for hedging. In our view superior to Leyland Cypress, but slower growing. Good for parks and gardens, its shiny, green foliage smells of pineapple when crushed.

20+
Mature height: 20m+

Shape of mature tree

Hedging trees

Telephone 01353 720 748 • www.barcham.co.uk • Fax 01353 723 060

# TILIA americana Redmond

This cultivar of the American Lime is of garden origin, and came from Plumfield Nurseries Nebraska, USA, in 1927. It was originally listed under Tilia euchlora but is distinctly different. It is still little known and used in the UK but should not be overlooked.

A pyramidal tree of medium size, this cultivar is barely sensitive to aphids and the associated "dripping", which makes it an ideal lime for street and avenue plantings. The super large leaves, which are a lighter green than those of the species, turn pale yellow in autumn.

| Mature height: 10-15m | Shape of mature tree | Avenue trees |

# TILIA cordata
## *Small-leaved Lime*

This well known native tree won the Award of Garden Merit in 2002 and remains a popular choice within our urban and rural landscapes. It is a good host to mistletoe for the more romantically inclined of you.

**This large tree has a broadly oval crown, with small, heart shaped leaves, which are dark green on top and pale green beneath. Its creamy white flowers are produced in July. It is a relatively sedate grower, is good for avenues and parks, and bears air pollution very well. Like most Lime, it is also a fine candidate for pollarding or pleaching.**

| Mature height: 20m+ | Shape of mature tree | Parkland trees |

# TILIA cordata Greenspire

**This American clone derived from the cultivar 'Euclid'. A selection from the Boston Parks, it has been in cultivation in the UK since the early 1960s. A winner of the Award of Garden Merit in 2002, it is a very popular choice for urban planting where its uniformity is preferred over the native Tilia cordata.**

It maintains a strong leader and well branched crown through to maturity, which distinguishes it over other selections, as the premier clone of Tilia cordata. It thrives well on most soils and copes readily with harsh urban environments given enough soil to exploit. At maturity I would liken it to a great example of Tilia cordata at the same size but with Greenspire you get this every time. Clonal selections give uniformity whereas seed grown trees have a significant degree of genetic variation.

Mature height:
10-15m

Shape of
mature tree

Avenue
trees

Telephone 01353 720 748 ● www.barcham.co.uk ● Fax 01353 723 060

# TILIA cordata Rancho

This often overlooked variety is of lesser overall stature than 'Greenspire' but it can be considered neater, with the added bonus of a great and fragrant floral display in early summer. Its branch angles are mechanically strong. It was introduced into the UK in the early 1960s.

Ideal for urban plantings, streets and avenues, this medium tree has a dense, conical habit, and has very shiny, small leaves. Its compact and uniform growing qualities make it ideal for avenue planting, but it is not as well known as Greenspire so rarely gets specified. We rate this clone very highly and it thrives on most soils.

Mature height: 10-15m | Shape of mature tree | Urban trees

# TILIA cordata Winter Orange

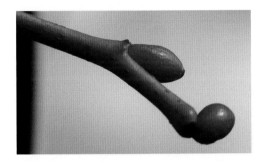

This exiting new variety was found as a seedling in the Netherlands in the 1970s. Whenever we show this tree it is widely appreciated and we never seem to have enough to go around! An ideal prospect for garden pleaching, its orange stems are most unusual.

A medium to large tree with a broadly oval crown, it is distinguished by its red buds and orange shoots in winter. Its white, sweetly scented flowers appear in July. It is a good choice for avenues and tolerates the rigours of the urban environment.

Mature height: 10-15m | Shape of mature tree | Garden trees

# TILIA x euchlora

*Caucasian Lime*

The result of a cross between Tilia cordata and Tilia dasystyla, this ever popular lime can grow as broad as it is tall, so is often given the wrong sites to grow on. Its flowers can have a narcotic effect on bees, which can sometimes be found on the ground near a tree. Redeemingly, it is free of aphids, so an ideal tree for pleaching or boxing in hard areas.

This Lime reacts well to pollarding, which is a good way of controlling its broadly pendulous habit. It is a medium to large tree, and as aphids are not attracted to its dark green foliage, the associated "stickiness" is not a problem. Good for wide verges, parks, avenues and urban plantings.

Mature height: 15-20m    Shape of mature tree    Urban trees

# TILIA x europaea

*Common Lime*

Once the most frequently planted Lime, this is a very long lived tree and commonly planted in central Europe as an urban tree. It is a hybrid between Tilia cordata and Tilia platyphyllos and has been known to reach over 50 metres tall, like the specimen at Duncombe Park in Yorkshire.

A large and impressive, oval shaped tree which is widely used for avenue plantings. It is recognisable by its dense suckering, which forms burrs on the trunk. Its large lush leaves can attract aphids so care should be taken not to plant in hard areas, where the resulting sooty mound will be a problem.

Mature height: 20m+    Shape of mature tree    Avenue trees

● Telephone 01353 720 748 ● www.barcham.co.uk ● Fax 01353 723 060

# TILIA x europaea Pallida

## *Kaiser Linden*

The Kaiser Linden is the Lime of the famous Unter den Linden in Berlin and has been highly rated for many years. It is quick to grow and gives a uniform alternative against seed grown Common Lime that makes it perfect for large avenues.

A large tree of pyramidal form, its pale green leaves have attractive, green-yellow undersides. It thrives pretty much anywhere and is tolerant of most soils. Quick to grow and establish, this is one of our most popular selling limes but as with its parents, care should be taken to avoid hard areas that could be affected by aphid drip.

|  |  | |
|---|---|---|
| 20+ | | |
| Mature height: 20m+ | Shape of mature tree | Avenue trees |

# TILIA henryana

This rarely seen Lime was discovered in China in 1888 by Augustine Henry. It was introduced into the UK in 1901 by Ernest Wilson and for some reason is still heavily under grown. We are bucking this trend and have been bulking up production numbers, but have noticed that in young plants the growth tips can be frost sensitive, so we advise sheltered sites for final placement.

Its ovate leaves are downy to the touch on both sides, and edged with bristle-like teeth akin to the outer edges of a Venus Fly Trap. A wonderfully ornamental lime, it flowers in autumn, and is a good choice for south facing parks and gardens within the milder parts of the UK.

|  |  | |
|---|---|---|
| 10|15 | | |
| Mature height: 10-15m | Shape of mature tree | Garden trees |

# TILIA mongolica
## *Mongolian Lime*

The Mongolian Lime was introduced from its homeland in the early 1880s. It is both aphid resistant and most unlike the general look of the rest of the Tilia family. Recent plantings in London have been most encouraging, and suggest this has great potential for an urban tree in the UK.

This small tree with a rounded habit has all the durability of Lime, but is of a size which makes it ideal as a street tree. It has small, serrated, glossy, green leaves, which are similar to those of ivy. A real little beauty requiring little maintenance.

| 7|10 | | |
|---|---|---|
| Mature height: 7-10m | Shape of mature tree | Urban trees |

**It turns to a clear and delicate yellow in autumn and as the leaves are so small for a Lime in the first place, there is not much leaf litter to contend with for an urban environment.**

Telephone 01353 720 748  •  www.barcham.co.uk  •  Fax 01353 723 060

# TILIA platyphyllos

## *Broad-leaved Lime*

The Broad-leaved Lime is a native of Britain. A winner of the First Class Certificate in 1892, it flowers in June / July and is very tolerant of pruning. It is a compact and stocky tree, the luscious foliage always gives it a healthy demeanour. The clonal selection 'Delft' is a European clone that forms a more pyramidal crown at maturity and could be used where uniformity is required.

20+

Mature height:
20m+

Shape of
mature tree

Native
trees

## *Broad-leaved Lime*

A large, fast growing tree with a roughly fissured bark, which remains relatively free of suckers. This is a good subject for parks and estates, and is also useful for avenue planting. The leaves are almost circular and dark green. It is well suited to urban conditions but thrives best in our countryside.

# TILIA platyphyllos Rubra
## *Red-twigged Lime*

The Red-twigged Lime is a slow grower than its parent and its fresh red twiggy growth is particularly striking when used for pleaching. It has a more ascending habit that the species and it won the Award of Garden Merit in 2002.

This reasonably columnar, medium to large tree is a great choice for avenue planting and areas which suffer from air pollution. Its young shoots are a bright brown-red, and look particularly effective in late winter. It makes a fine choice for a rural landscape and will thrive on most soils given enough room.

| Mature height: 15-20m | Shape of mature tree | Avenue trees |

# TILIA tomentosa
## *Silver Lime*

**The Silver Lime is a handsome tree, but with a rather variable habit. Introduced in 1767 from its native South Eastern Europe, its flowers can be toxic to bees so this should be considered if planting in a rural setting.**

A large tree of generally pyramidal habit, the Silver Lime has the advantages of being resistant to both aphids and drought. It grows well in urban areas, although it requires plenty of space. Its dark green leaves have silver-white undersides, creating a beautiful effect when rustled by the breeze. Good for avenues and parks, it will also stand up well to salt-laden coastal winds.

| Mature height: 20m+ | Shape of mature tree | Urban trees |

# TILIA tomentosa Brabant

This Dutch clonal selection of Silver Lime was introduced into the UK in the early 1970s and won the Award of Garden Merit in 2002. It is rightly considered to be an excellent urban tree, coping with the rigours of city environments very well. The Belgium variety, 'Doornik' has very similar attributes.

Brabant has a more regularly pyramidal form than the species, but is just as large. It is very versatile, being suitable for urban settings, avenues, verges and parks. The striking silver undersides of its foliage makes it a wonderful tree for providing contrast within a landscape and the leaves turn a glorious yellow before falling in the autumn.

| Mature height: 20m+ | Shape of mature tree | Urban trees |

● Telephone 01353 720 748   ● www.barcham.co.uk   ● Fax 01353 723 060

# TILIA petiolaris
## *Weeping Silver Lime*

The Weeping Silver Lime is perhaps the most graceful of all large, weeping trees. Often referred to as Tilia tomentosa Petiolaris it has been recently separated to its own species but in my opinion this is too close to call so doesn't really matter anyway. There is a particularly good specimen to be seen at The RHS garden at Wisley.

Mature height: 20m+  |  Shape of mature tree  |  Parkland trees

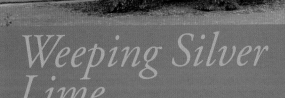

## *Weeping Silver Lime*

Introduced in the early 1840s it won the Award of Garden Merit in 2002. It is fast growing and aphid resistant, and is an excellent subject for parks. The flowers are richly scented but narcotic to bees, while its dark green leaves have white, felt-like undersides. Autumn colour is a striking and rich yellow. It thrives on most soils.

# TRACHYCARPUS fortunei

## *Chusan Palm*

A remarkable genus of hardy palm, introduced by Robert Fortune in 1849. Slow to grow, I have one in my garden that was planted at 60 cm tall, and now stands at a little over 2 metres ten years later. It won the Award of Garden Merit in 2002 and is the best hardy palm for the UK.

While it is hardy in Britain, we recommend planting it in sheltered positions to avoid wind damage to its deep green, fan shaped leaves. Its slender trunk becomes clothed in loose, dark brown fibres and small yellow flowers borne in large panicles are produced in early summer once the plant attains about 2 metres of height.

Mature height: 5-10m  |  Shape of mature tree  |  Garden trees

# ULMUS americana Princeton Riveredge

*Princeton Elm™*

An exciting addition to our range, with proven resistance to Dutch Elm disease. In two individual studies of the disease, spanning seven years, each conducted by research geneticists at the USDA National Arboretum, the Riveredge Princeton Elm scored at the top for tolerance and recovery to the massive doses of the most virulent strain. Recently planted as an avenue, lining the road outside the White House in America, we now pin our colours on this clone above others.

20+

Mature height: 20m+

Shape of mature tree

Avenue trees

We secured the UK rights to this cultivar when we partnered with Riveredge Farms in the States. This is the only Elm with a proven track record and there are thriving avenues in America that are over 80 years old. Its parents derive from trees dated at over 287 years old. It is a quick growing, broad leaved tree, rounded when young but developing a spreading open canopy at maturity. It will take a few years for us to bulk up numbers on this tree, but they are available on a limited basis. The first avenue planted in the UK was at Highgrove for Prince Charles. Much independent research has been undertaken on this clone in America and it is rated to have the best resistance by far. It is tolerant of most soils and also thrives on coastal sites.

Telephone 01353 720 748 ● www.barcham.co.uk ● Fax 01353 723 060

**Barcham**

U

# ULMUS carpinifolia Wredei Aurea

This rather slow growing Elm is probably protected against Dutch Elm disease as a result of its size rather than genetic makeup. A sport of 'Dampieri', it won the First Class Certificate in 1893.

A tree of small to medium size and oval habit, it tolerates pollution and salt-laden, coastal winds. Very good for parks, gardens and verges. Its luminescent yellow foliage is particularly striking if planted in a semi shaded area or against a dark backdrop.

Mature height: 5-10m    Shape of mature tree    Garden trees

---

# ULMUS glabra Camperdownii

*Camperdown Elm*

**The Camperdown Elm is a form of Wych Elm. The original appeared at Camperdown House, near Dundee, in 1850. It produces clusters of attractive hop like flowers in the spring and its lustrous leaves add well to its effect.**

A small weeping tree with a dome shaped head; it looks good growing in a lawn in parks and gardens. It remains neat and compact, and is generally considered to be resistant to Dutch elm disease but only because it doesn't attain the height to attract the infecting beetle.

Mature height: 5-10m    Shape of mature tree    Garden trees

262

# ULMUS Clusius

**This Dutch hybrid was raised at Wageningen and released for general cultivation in 1983. It is derived from the same parents as Ulmus Lobel, namely Ulmus glabra Exoniensis and Ulmus wallichiana.**

This large broadly oval tree is fast growing and well suited to avenue and coastal plantings. It has a resistance to Dutch elm disease but is more susceptible than 'Princeton'.

20+
Mature height: 20m+

Shape of mature tree

Parkland trees

# ULMUS Dodoens

This Elm was seed-raised in the 1950s and eventually released for general cultivation in 1973. It has the same parents as 'Clusius' and has moderate resistance to Dutch elm disease.

This tough large tree, which is good for verges and avenues, forms a broadly pyramidal crown. It is fast growing and a good choice for windy, exposed locations including coastal sites.

20+
Mature height: 20m+

Shape of mature tree

Parkland trees

# ULMUS Lobel

This Elm cultivar was raised at Wageningen in the Netherlands, and was selected for its resistance to Dutch elm disease. It has the same parentage as 'Clusius' and was released for general cultivation in 1973.

Large and fast growing, this narrow, columnar tree eventually becomes broader. It will withstand exposed locations, including those on coasts, and is also good for avenues and verges.

20
Mature height: 20m

Shape of mature tree

Urban trees

# ZELKOVA serrata

**A relative of the Elm, this is a native of Japan. Introduced into the UK in 1861, it won the Award of Garden Merit in 2002. It thrives on most soils and is well suited to tolerate the rigours of the urban environment.**

This is a medium to large tree with a wide spreading and rounded habit. Its smooth, grey bark flakes attractively, and its foliage displays fine shades of red and bronze in autumn. Good for avenues and parkland. Zelkovas do best in fertile, sandy, loamy soils.

| 15\|20 | | |
|---|---|---|
| Mature height: 15-20m | Shape of mature tree | Parkland trees |

# ZELKOVA serrata Green Vase

This is a recent American introduction brought into the UK in the 1980s and is widely viewed as the best clonal selection available. It is quick to grow, especially in the first ten years or so, after which it becomes more sedate.

The much tighter, columnar habit of this medium to large cultivar makes it considerably more suitable as a street tree than the species. It also tolerates air pollution and windy sites. The trunk has a soft grey bark and foliage provides very good autumn colour. It thrives on most soils.

| 15\|20 | | |
|---|---|---|
| Mature height: 15-20m | Shape of mature tree | Parkland trees |

# ZIZIPHUS guiggiolo

*Chinese Date*

We were introduced to this variety after our Sales Director saw it on his holiday in Southern Spain. Thought to have been cultivated for its fruit in China some 4000 years ago and still popular today.

Originating from China, where it is grown as a commercial fruiting crop, it makes a small dome shaped tree. Russet brown dates of about 2-3 centimetres are profusely borne by late summer, but the tree can sucker, so it is unsuitable for paved / hard areas. Being a desert species it is very tolerant of drought and its thorny stems add to a pleasing architectural effect. A collector's item!!

| 5 | | |
|---|---|---|
| Mature height: 5m | Shape of mature tree | Garden trees |

Telephone 01353 720 748   •   www.barcham.co.uk   •   Fax 01353 723 060

# Trees for a purpose

### Choosing the right tree to suit your environment

● Telephone 01353 720 748   ● www.barcham.co.uk   ● Fax 01353 723 060

## Evergreen Trees

## Extreme PH, acid or alkaline

## Flowering

## Garden

## Hedging

## Narrow Trees

## Parkland trees

# Trees for a purpose continued

## Red / Purple Leaves

## Stilted Screening

## Urban Trees

## Variegated Trees

## Weeping Trees

## Wet Soils

## Yellow Foliage

Telephone 01353 720 748   •   www.barcham.co.uk   •   Fax 01353 723 060